The ABC's of the IBM PC

The ABC's of the IBM® PC

Joan Lasselle
Carol Ramsay

Berkeley • Paris • Düsseldorf SYBEX®

Cover art by Sato Yamomoto
Design and illustration by Gaynelle B. Grover

Library of Congress Card Number: 83-63019
ISBN 0-89588-102-0
First Edition 1984
Printed in the United States of America
10 9 8 7 6 5 4 3 2 1

Table of Contents

Acknowledgements

We would like to thank Michael McGrath and Joyce Cox for their support and editorial expertise in producing this book.

Introduction

Whether you have just purchased an IBM Personal Computer to use at home or whether you found one on your desk when you arrived at work this morning, this book is for you, the IBM PC user.

We assume that you have little or no experience with PCs (or any other computer), and that you are not going to write your own programs—at least, not right away. Rather you will be using purchased programs, called applications, such as VisiCalc or WordStar. You are anxious to learn the basics and put your PC to work. But where do you start?

For those of you who have been frustrated and baffled—the IBM PC *Guide to Operations* in one hand and the *DOS Reference Manual* in the other—we have written this step-by-step guide that will have you loading, entering, saving, and retrieving in no time.

This book is designed to get you started. Because you learn best by doing, we include exercises so that you can practice on your own PC as we go along. Here are the things we are going to talk about:

Chapter 1—Introduces you to the parts of your PC: the hardware and the software. It identifies and describes the function of each component and discusses the different kinds of software applications you will probably be using.

Chapter 2—Gets you started. You turn on the PC, load the operating system, and set the date and time.

Chapter 3—Shows you how to communicate with your PC using simple commands, menu selections, and function keys.

Chapter 4—Tells you all about using diskettes. It includes proper handling, storage, labeling, and protection of diskettes. In addition you will learn how to copy them.

Chapter 5—Tells you about files and the way information is stored on diskettes. You learn to name, list, copy, rename, and delete files.

Chapter 6—Discusses application programs in general.

Chapter 7—Introduces you to WordStar and VisiCalc. Two short work sessions give you a feel for word processing and spreadsheets.

Chapter 8—Describes additional components you can add to your PC to perform special functions, such as printing, graphics, and communications.

Chapter 9—Gives you a checklist for problem solving if things do not go as planned.

In addition, there are two appendices that tell you how to unpack and set up your PC and how to perform all the exercises on a single-drive PC, and two more appendices that give a glossary of terms and a list of resources.

What You Will Need

To use this book most successfully, you will need:

- An IBM PC so you can perform the operations as they are described;
- A copy of the DOS operating system (sometimes called PC-DOS). This is purchased separately from your IBM dealer; and
- A little time. We have given you only the essentials—you will still need some time to try it all out.

This book assumes you are using version 1.1 of the DOS operating system. The information we present here is also correct for versions 1.0 or 2.0. If you are using one of these operating systems, however, the messages displayed on the screen may be different or a file we ask you to use may not be available. In either case, you can still do the exercises as they are described, but use the examples we give you as models rather than performing them exactly.

If you want to sit down and use your IBM PC for the first time, you are probably faced with one of two situations: the PC is cabled, connected, plugged in, and ready to go; or you are looking at a couple of large cardboard boxes and wondering where to start. If you need help putting your computer together, go to *Appendix A* where we tell you everything you need to know about setting up your PC.

Once that is done, you are ready for *Chapter 1,* which introduces you to the parts of your PC and talks about the different ways you can use it.

one

A

Anatomy of Your PC

You probably already know that computers consist of both hardware and software. The hardware is the machine itself; the software is the information you use with it. A useful analogy is your stereo system; the stereo components are the equivalent of your computer's hardware and the record albums and tapes are the equivalent of software.

Let's begin by identifying the hardware components of your PC.

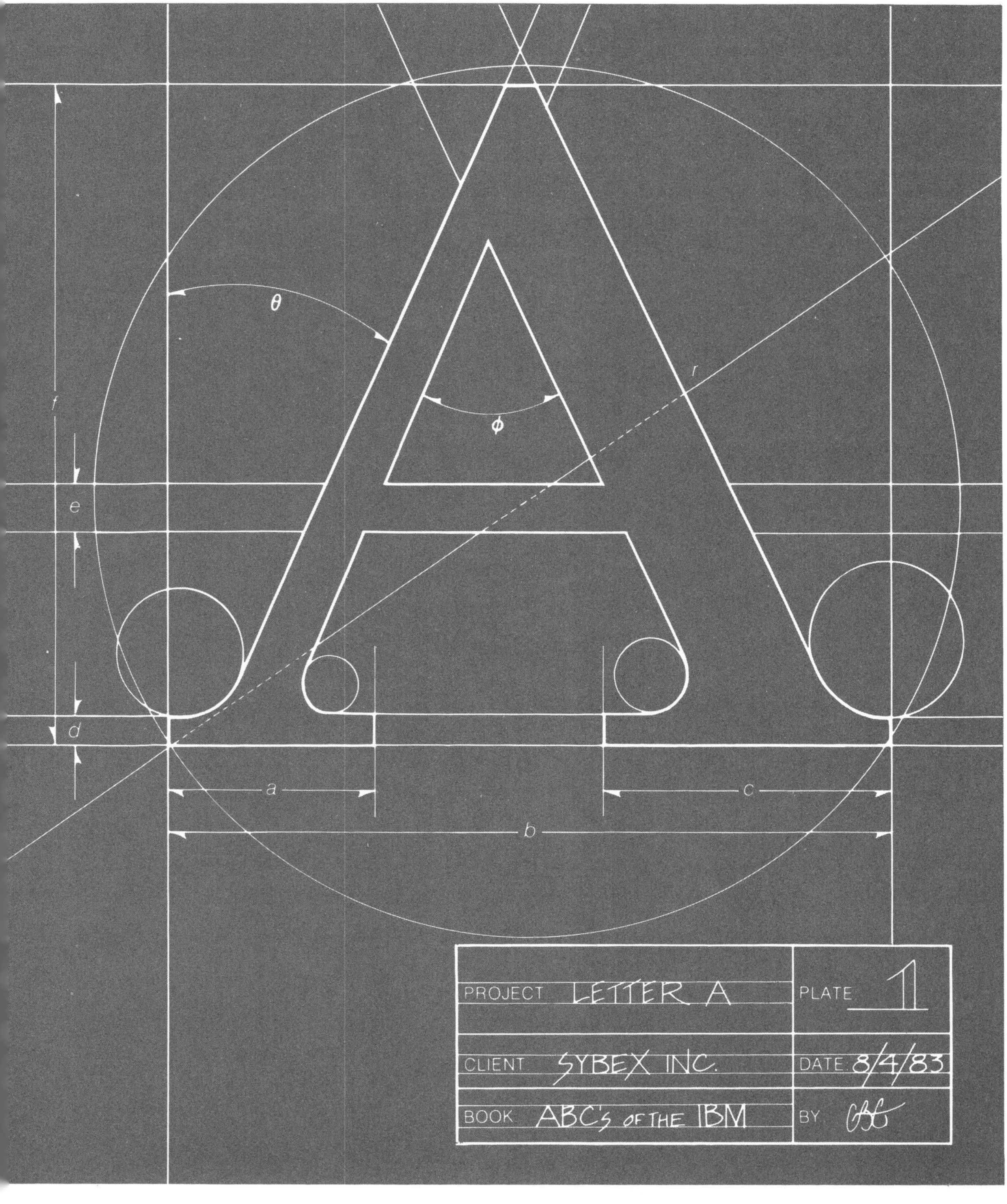
θ
φ
r
f
e
d
a
b
c
PROJECT LETTER A
PLATE 1
CLIENT SYBEX INC.
DATE 8/4/83
BOOK ABC's OF THE IBM
BY

HARDWARE

The System Unit

The system unit is really the computer itself. It performs all operations, calculations, and processes; that is why it is often called the Central Processing Unit or CPU. Inside are the electronic components, the microprocessor and printed-circuit boards that make the PC work.

The system unit contains the PC's memory. Memory is what we call the device that stores information and instructions. Some information and instructions are stored permanently, and some are loaded into memory from a diskette to be stored in memory temporarily. Temporary storage can be programs, such as the operating system or application software, or it can be the reports or information you use with the programs. Since your PC's memory capacity is limited, these programs and data are stored on diskettes when they are not being used, so that they do not take up valuable memory space.

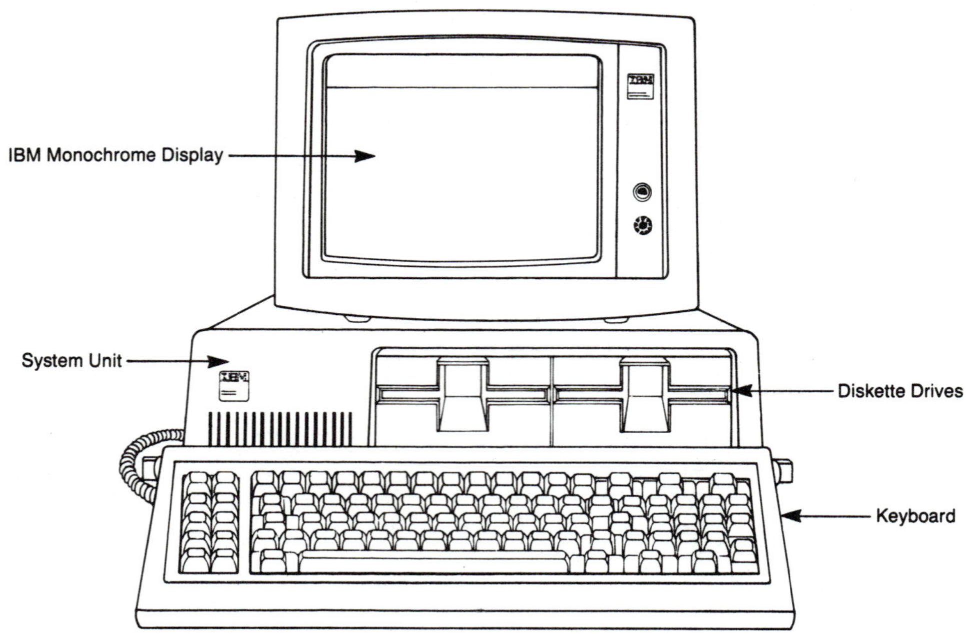

Figure 1.1: The IBM Personal Computer

The Keyboard

You communicate with your PC by typing instructions and pressing keys on the keyboard. You will notice that the central part of the keyboard is just like a typewriter. The keys in the areas to the right and left are used to perform special operations, sometimes alone and sometimes in conjunction with other keys.

If you are familiar with a typewriter or other keyboard, you know that one key sometimes serves two purposes. For example, you type 5 if you want a 5 but you hold down the Shift key and type 5 if you want a % sign. Many keys on the PC keyboard are used like the Shift key, giving different results when used with another key. You will learn about these keys throughout this book, especially in *Chapter 3.*

The keyboard itself is designed to be tilted or level, and is easily adjusted with the knobs on either side.

It may surprise you to know that the basic PC consists of only the system unit and keyboard—no diskette drive, no display. However, in this form, you cannot store information and you cannot see what you type on the keyboard, so some kind of storage and a display are essential additions.

The Diskette Drives

Diskette drives are the mechanisms that transfer information. When you insert a diskette in a diskette drive, you can transfer information from the diskette into memory (loading) or from memory to the diskette (saving, storing, or writing). This is similar to recording and playing back a tape or record album. You can actually connect an audio cassette recorder to the basic PC and use it to store information. However, most people purchase their PC with one or two diskette drives, which provides a much more efficient way of storing and retrieving information.

There are advantages to having two diskette drives. For example, when you want to copy information from one diskette to another, the diskette you are copying from goes in one drive and the diskette you are copying to goes in the other. The copying operation is then carried out in one step. With only one drive, you begin to make the copy, stop to change diskettes, then complete the operation. Another example: When you use an application program, the program diskette can go in one drive and a diskette for storing information can go in the other. With only one drive, you have to stop to change diskettes when you want to store or load information.

Having only one diskette drive does not limit what you can do; it just takes a little longer and requires more swapping around of diskettes for some operations.

This book assumes that you have two diskette drives. The one on the left is called A:, and the one on the right is called B:. They are not labeled, so you will just have to remember which is which. However, you will use them so often that remembering won't be much of a problem.

If you have a single-drive system, you will find instructions for completing the exercises in *Appendix B*.

The Display

Different people call the display by different names. You might hear it referred to as a monitor, console, CRT (Cathode Ray Tube), VDU (Video Display Unit), terminal, or, simply, screen. Whatever you call it, its function is to display what you type on the keyboard, to give you instructions, and to ask you questions.

Your computer does not need a display to do its job, but *you* need it so that you have an idea of what is going on. Without a display, you do not know what you are typing and your PC has no way to communicate with you. A display is really more of a necessity than an option, although it is purchased separately. For simplicity, we assume that you have an IBM Monochrome Display, but you can

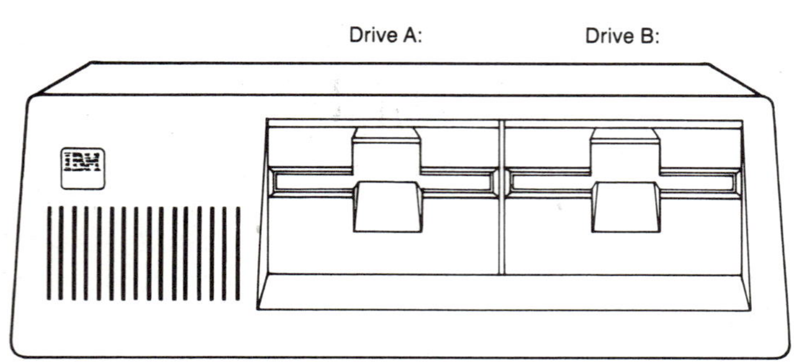

Figure 1.2: Drive Identifiers A: and B:

use other displays, including a regular home TV set. If you want to use the PC with your TV set, you will have to buy a special adapter, called an RF modulator, to convert the signal that the PC puts out into one that the TV can understand. Consult your *Guide to Operations* for more information.

The knobs on the front of the IBM display are used to adjust the contrast and brightness of the screen, just like a TV.

SOFTWARE

You will be using three kinds of software with your PC: the disk operating system; application programs; and the information and reports you create with the application programs. This software is stored on diskettes.

The Disk Operating System

The disk operating system coordinates the transfer of information between the memory in the system unit and the diskette (which is sometimes called external memory). It also coordinates other activities such as printing.

Your IBM PC uses an operating system called DOS or PC-DOS—you cannot operate your computer without it. You do not automatically receive a copy of DOS when you purchase your PC. You have to buy it separately.

Application Programs

Application programs operate in conjunction with DOS so that you can perform useful tasks with your PC without having to be a programmer. There are thousands of application programs available that convert your PC into a tool to increase productivity and decrease paperwork. The most popular ones can be grouped into five categories: word processors, spreadsheets, database management programs, payroll and accounting programs, and graphics. A sixth category, games, converts your PC into an entertainment center.

Chances are, if you are using your PC at home or in the office, you will be using one or more of these kinds of programs. So let's take a look at what each of them can do for you.

Word Processors

Word processors turn your PC into a super typewriter. The two most popular word-processing programs are WordStar and EasyWriter—we introduce you to WordStar in *Chapter 7.*

With a word processor you compose text using your PC keyboard just as you would use a typewriter keyboard. However, because the characters are recorded electronically rather than on paper, you can correct your mistakes and make any changes you want before printing the text out on a printer. You can erase words, phrases, or whole blocks of text, insert new ones, or move them from one place to another with a few keystrokes. Then you can store your document on a diskette and go back to it at any time. You can print it or revise it whenever you want, or you can copy it and store multiple versions of the same document.

One of the real benefits of some word-processing programs is that you can view your document on your PC's display before printing it out. If you don't like what you see, you can change margins, line spacing, or tab settings and see the effect immediately on the screen. This is called on-screen formatting. You see only the portion of the document that can fit on your screen at one time, but that does not mean that the size of your document is limited to the size of your screen. You can move backwards and forwards through the document as you wish, looking at a page or section at a time. This is called paging or scrolling.

In some offices, a few PCs may be used only for word processing. These dedicated machines are probably in the hands of secretaries who can really make them produce. However, because of word processing, typing is no longer just for secretaries. Many office professionals use word processors to compose reports or letters and to jot off memos or notes. In addition, a large group of professional writers feel that their wildest dreams have come true!

Spreadsheets

We talk about spreadsheets in more detail in *Chapter 7,* so we will just give you a brief introduction here.

All electronic spreadsheets are based on the same idea. You are given an electronic worksheet or grid made up of rows and columns. The intersection of each row and column is called a cell. You can set up a typical financial report or model by entering column and row labels such as Sales, Expenses, or Profit and the appropriate data—either numbers or formulas. The numbers represent variables and the formulas maintain their relationship between the variables. If the values (numbers) change, all related values change. If you change a variable value, all related values change on the basis of the formula. If you change the relationship by changing the formula, again all affected entries are changed.

Spreadsheets make it easy to play the *What If?* game. Once your model is established, you can use it to see the potential effect of different decisions. What if expenses increase? What if sales decrease? What about expanding? Where is the breakeven point? At home, you can analyze stock purchase decisions, figure your income tax, or decide whether it is more cost effective to rent or buy that piece of equipment.

VisiCalc is currently the most popular spreadsheet. However, its popularity has spawned lots of similar products, many of which you can use with your PC.

Database Management Programs

Databases are large pools of information, which can be numbers or text. You can use a database management program to search for a particular piece of information, to find all information in the database fitting certain criteria, or to sort the information in specified ways. Databases can be used with other programs such as word processors or spreadsheets.

Databases can be extremely large, such as one an airline uses for issuing passengers' tickets, or very small, such as one that keeps a list of the employees in your department.

Two popular database programs are Personal Filing System and dBase II. Both of these programs allow you to collect and categorize information, and then retrieve it in different forms. However, they each do some things better than others, so you need to pick the product best suited to your project.

Payroll and Accounting Programs

If you run a small business, you can use an accounting application for your payroll, accounts payable and receivable, and general ledger. If you have the kind of business where everyone wears lots of hats, computerized accounting can free up time to focus on the business of the business rather than the bookkeeping.

In the past many small businesses have bought accounting services from a bank or computer service center. With a PC, you can buy an application program and do your own accounting, probably for less money.

Graphics

Graphics programs let you display information as a graph or chart. You can display pie charts, bar and line graphs, or scattergrams. Graphics programs make it easy to summarize large amounts of data or to identify trends. Often graphs are used in reports or as presentation aids.

Graphics programs are very useful; however, they require special hardware. For example, you must add a special graphics board to your system unit as well as a graphics monitor (usually a color monitor). In addition, you may want to buy a plotter so that you can make a copy on paper of the graph or chart that is displayed on your screen.

Games

At home, games are a popular use for the PC. Like everything else, some are good and some are bad—the choice is pretty broad. Some of the best games include animation and lively graphics as well as different levels of expertise.

While games do not generally help get the job done at the office, they are good forms of relaxation and some people feel they sharpen problem-solving skills and hand-eye coordination.

Now that you know what you will be working with in terms of both hardware and software, you are ready to begin using your PC.

REVIEW

Your computer has the following hardware components:

- The system unit.
- The keyboard.
- The diskette drives.
- The display.

There are three kinds of software:

- Disk operating systems.
- Application programs.
- The reports and information you use with your application programs.

There are six common types of application programs:

- Word processors.
- Spreadsheets.
- Database management programs.
- Payroll and accounting programs.
- Graphics.
- Games.

two

B

Beginning with the Basics

Now that you are familiar with the parts of your IBM Personal Computer and have an idea of some of the things you can do with it, you are ready to start using your PC for the first time. But before you go any further, check two things:

- Is your PC plugged in?
- Do you have a copy of DOS? (You will find it in the back of the *DOS Reference Manual*.)

Yes to both questions? Then you are ready to proceed with this chapter. If you have not yet purchased a copy of DOS, plan to do so immediately. You cannot do anything except admire your PC until you have DOS.

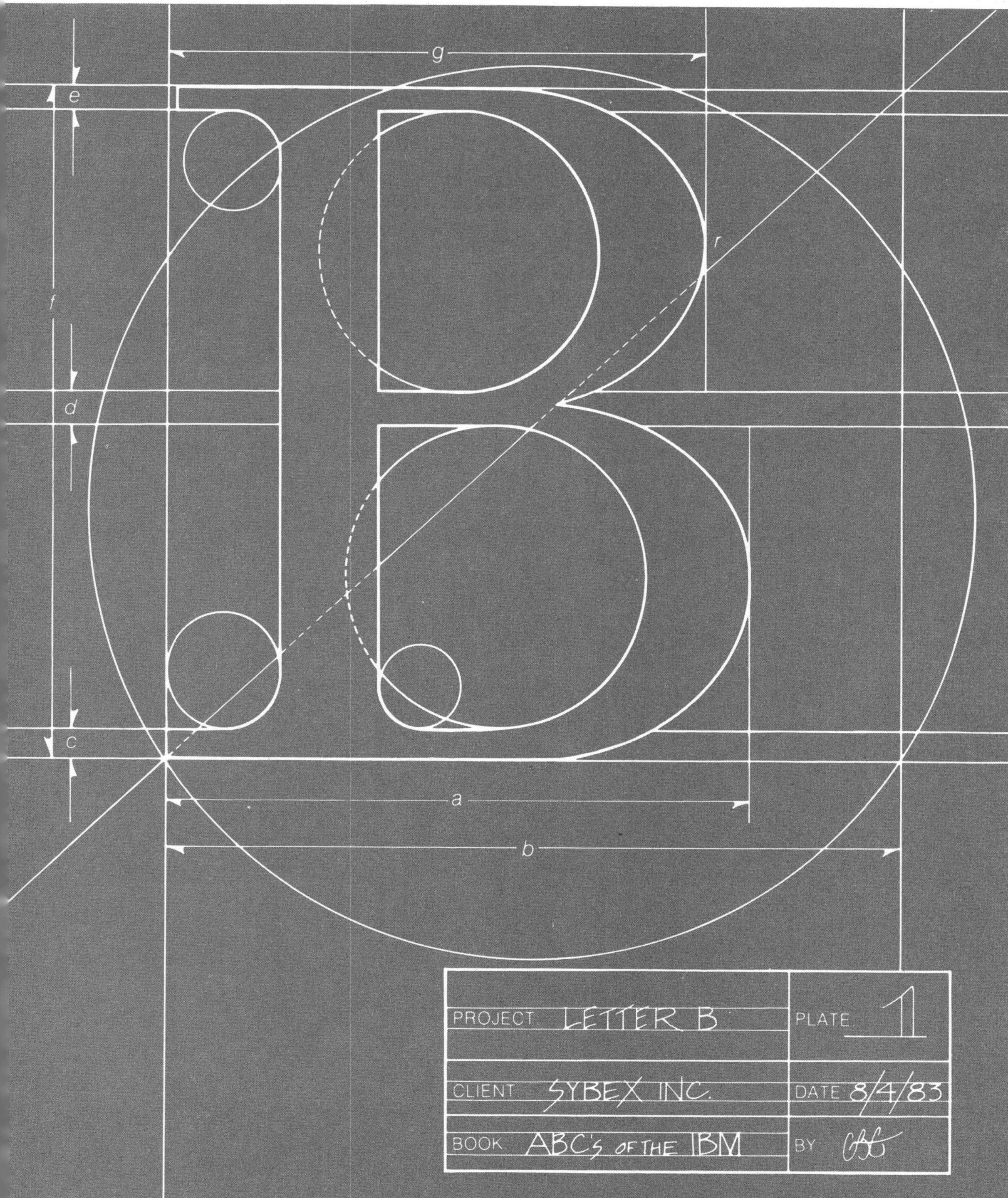
g
e
f
d
c
r
a
b
PROJECT: LETTER B
PLATE: 1
CLIENT: SYBEX INC.
DATE: 8/4/83
BOOK: ABC's OF THE IBM
BY:

TURNING ON YOUR PC

Turning on your PC is just a matter of following these steps:

1. Turn the knobs on the front of the display fully to the right. These are the contrast and brightness knobs. Once your PC is warmed up, you can adjust them, but if you don't start with them fully on, you might not see anything on the screen.
2. Turn on the power with the switch on the right side of the system unit.

When you first turn on your PC, it runs through a quick test to make sure everything is in working order. If the test is successful, three things happen:

1. After the system warms up (this takes a few moments), a blinking underscore called the cursor appears at the top left of the screen.
2. You hear a short beep.
3. This message appears at the top of the screen:

```
IBM Personal Computer Basic
Version C1.00 Copyright IBM Corp 1981
62940 Bytes free
Ok

_
```

At the bottom of the screen there are some numbers and labels that we will explain later (page 31).

LOADING DOS

As we have said, DOS is the disk operating system for the IBM PC. It is stored on a diskette that you will find in the back of your *DOS Reference Manual*. To use your PC, you have to load DOS. Loading something into your computer (whether it is DOS or other software, such as an application program) means having your computer copy information from a diskette into its memory. The information remains on the diskette; it is only copied into memory.

You can load DOS in one of two ways: by inserting the diskette and turning on the power, or, if the power is already on, by inserting the diskette and resetting the PC. When you reset, you clear the information currently stored in memory and read in new information from another diskette. The information you load remains in the PC's memory until you either reset the computer again or turn off the power.

Assuming your PC is still turned on, follow these steps to load DOS.

1. Remove the DOS diskette, still inside its protective paper sleeve, from the plastic holder in the back of the *DOS Reference Manual*.
2. Hold the diskette with the label up, right thumb on the label, and slide it out of its paper sleeve. Be careful not to touch the surfaces that are exposed through the cutouts on the diskette jacket. (If you are lost already, take a look at the drawing below.)
3. Open the door of drive A: (the left-hand drive) if it is not already open.

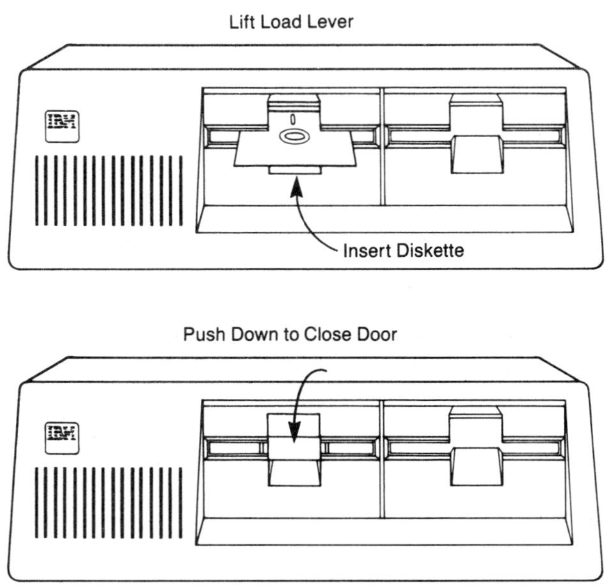

Figure 2.1: Inserting a Diskette

4. Push the diskette gently into the drive, being careful not to bend it. Make sure it is fully inserted.
5. Close the drive door.
6. Reset your PC by holding down the Ctrl and Alt keys on the left of the keyboard, and pressing the Del key on the right. (Lost again? Figure 2.2 will help you locate these keys. For now, you need not worry about what each individual key does.)
7. The cursor blinks at the top of the screen, the red drive light goes on, and you hear some whirrs and clicks that tell you that DOS is being loaded into your computer.
8. Then you see the current-date message. For example:

```
Current date is Tue 1-01-1980
Enter new date: _
```

The Cursor

The blinking underscore you see after *date*: is called the cursor. It marks the position on the screen where the next character you type will appear. You will see the cursor move about as you enter and change information. In a moment, we will tell you how to make the cursor move wherever you want it to (page 20).

Now you are ready to go on.

Figure 2.2: The Ctrl, Alt, and Del Keys

SETTING THE DATE AND TIME

Every time you load DOS, it asks you for the current date and time. You do not have to set them, but setting them now can prove useful later on.

When you store information on a diskette, if you have set the date and time at the beginning of the session, DOS automatically stores the precise date and time with the information. Should you have more than one version of the same information, you can check the date later to see which version is most current. If you have not set the date, the existing date will be used as the date for every file.

You can use several formats for the date and time, but some are not acceptable. For example, July 4th will not work since DOS accepts only numbers in the date.

The most common way to enter the date is month/day/year, as in 4/12/83, though 4-12-83 is also acceptable. Time is usually entered as hours:minutes or hours:minutes:seconds, as in 10:05 or 15:45:24. You can also add hundredths of seconds. Refer to your *DOS Reference Manual* for a list of all the acceptable formats.

If you use a format that is not acceptable, DOS flashes *Invalid date* or *Invalid time* on the screen and lets you try again.

Set the date and time now, following these steps:

1. Your PC is waiting for you to enter a new date so go ahead and type in today's date immediately after *Enter new date:*. For example:

```
Enter new date:12-25-83
```

Correcting Mistakes

If you make a mistake, press the Backspace key (←) to go back to the point of the error and retype correctly. Notice that each time you press ←, the character to the left of the cursor is erased and the cursor moves back one space. In this way, you can backspace over an error to erase it, then retype the correct characters. If you are a perfect typist, you might want to make some deliberate mistakes so that you can practice erasing them.

Figure 2.3: The Backspace Key (⟵)

Entering What You Have Typed

The Enter key (↵) on your PC keyboard replaces the Return key on a typewriter keyboard. Sometimes you will use it like the Return key, but usually you will use it to enter an instruction into the computer. Although the information you type on the keyboard is displayed on the screen, the computer has no knowledge of it until you enter it by pressing ↵ to finalize the operation.

2. When you are satisfied that your typing is flawless, enter the date by pressing ↵ .

3. If you do not want to set the date, just press ↵ without typing anything.

4. Your PC displays the current-time message. For example:

```
Current time is: 0:00:47.94
Enter new time: _
```

5. Type the time after *Enter new time:*. For example:

```
Enter new time:15:30:00
```

6. If you typed the time correctly, press ↵ to enter it.

7. If you do not want to set the time, just press ↵ without typing anything.

Figure 2.4: The Enter Key (⟵┘)

8. At this point the DOS copyright statement and prompt appear on the screen. They look like this:

   ```
   The IBM Personal Computer DOS
   Version 1.10 (c) Copyright IBM Corp 1981, 1982
   A>
   ```

The DOS Prompt

Once DOS is loaded and the date and time are set, your screen displays *A>*. This is the DOS prompt, sometimes called the A prompt, and it tells you that DOS has been loaded successfully.

The A tells you that DOS is using drive A: as the current drive—unless you tell it otherwise, it will always expect to find the information it needs on a diskette in drive A:. The > symbol says *OK, I'm ready. Tell me what to do next.* That is why it is called a prompt; it is prompting you for the next instruction.

CHANGING THE CURRENT DRIVE

Remember that you inserted your DOS diskette into drive A:? If you have two diskette drives, you might decide to put another diskette in drive B: and start working with it instead. In that case, there would be no point in keeping drive A: as the current drive.

To move to drive B:, you are going to have to type a B:. Use the shift key to type a colon (:) just as you would on a typewriter.

The Shift Keys

The ⇧ keys on your PC keyboard replace the Shift keys on a typewriter keyboard. As with a typewriter, you can use them to type capital letters, symbols such as %, and some punctuation marks, including :.

Now practice moving from one drive to another.

1. The last line on your screen reads:

   A>_

   You move to drive B: by typing B: ↵ immediately after A>. The last line now reads:

   A>B:

   This changes the DOS prompt to B> and tells DOS to look at the diskette in drive B: for further instructions. This is sometimes called logging onto drive B: and drive B: then becomes the logged drive.

2. When you are ready to go back to drive A:, immediately after B> type A: ↵. The last line now reads:

   B>A:

   The DOS prompt A> reappears, indicating that drive A: is the current (or logged) drive once again.

Figure 2.5: The Shift Keys (⇧)

GETTING FAMILIAR WITH THE KEYBOARD

As you have realized by now, you communicate with your IBM PC by typing on the keyboard. You can enter commands and information, respond to prompts, and select different options or functions. All your word-processing and spreadsheet reports will be entered from the keyboard, as well as any information you want to use with other application programs.

Your PC keyboard is arranged very similarly to a typewriter keyboard. Most of the keys are marked just as they are on a typewriter with a few notable exceptions. You already know about the Enter key (↵), the Backspace key (←), and the Shift key (⇧). The Tab key, which works like a typewriter Tab key, is marked ⇆. But what are all those other keys?

There are three additional sets of keys on the PC keyboard that you will not find on a typewriter keyboard: the numeric keypad (which includes the cursor-positioning (arrow) keys), the function keys, and several control keys, the most important of which, for right now, is the Ctrl key.

The Numeric Keypad and the Arrow Keys

When you press the key marked Num Lock, you can use the numeric keypad located on the right of your keyboard to enter numbers. If you are going to use application programs that require lots of numbers, the numeric pad can be very handy, especially if you

Figure 2.6: The Numeric Keypad, the Arrow Keys, and the Num Lock Key

already know how to operate a ten-key calculator by touch.

When the Num Lock key is off (simply press it again to turn it off), you can use the keys marked with an arrow to position the cursor. The arrow keys move the cursor up, down, to the right, and to the left. You can also use the keys marked HOME, PG UP, PG DOWN, and END to move the cursor. These keys can have a special meaning for different application programs you may be using. Be sure to consult the reference manual for that program to find out what they mean.

The Function Keys

The ten function keys are grouped together on the left of your keyboard and are labeled F1 to F10. These keys perform predefined tasks that change from application to application. We will tell you more about them when we show you how to tell your PC what to do (page 31).

The Ctrl Key

Remember that we said in *Chapter 1* that some keys are used with other keys to add another dimension to your keyboard? For example, the key marked *j* becomes *J* when used with the Shift key. The Ctrl key works the same way. In the WordStar word-processing program, for example, the *j* key used with the Ctrl key gives you access to all kinds of helpful information.

Figure 2.7: The Function Keys

Figure 2.8: The Ctrl Key

So that starts you out. You always turn on the machine, load DOS, and optionally set the date and time to begin. These steps will become second nature soon, but until they do, here is a quick review of the points in this chapter.

REVIEW

To turn on the computer:

- Be sure the power cord is connected to the system unit and plugged into a live outlet.
- Turn on the power switch on the right side of the system unit.

To adjust the keyboard and screen brightness:

- Use the knobs on the side of the keyboard to tilt or lower the keyboard.
- Use the knobs on the front of the display screen to adjust the brightness and contrast.

To load DOS (power off):

- Insert the DOS diskette in drive A:.
- Turn on the machine.

To load DOS (power already on):

- Insert the DOS diskette in drive A:.
- Hold down the Ctrl and Alt keys while pressing the Del key to reset the computer.

About the date and time:

- Can be reset every time you load DOS.
- Saved with any files you store on diskette.
- Allow you to check for the most current information.

To correct mistakes:

- Use the Backspace key (←).

To enter what you have typed:

- Use the Enter key (↵).

To change the current drive:

- Type the drive identifier (A or B) followed by a : (for example, B:).

Three additional sets of keys:

- The numeric keypad (including the cursor-positioning (arrow) keys).
- The function keys.
- The Ctrl key.

three

C

Commands for Your PC

Your IBM PC is a willing servant provided you tell it exactly what you want it to do. Today's reality doesn't let you talk to your PC directly; however, you can communicate easily and effectively by using commands.

Commands are typed directly, selected from a list of command options, or chosen by pressing the function key associated with the command. The method depends on the software that you are using. For example, DOS, your computer's operating system, responds to commands that you type directly.

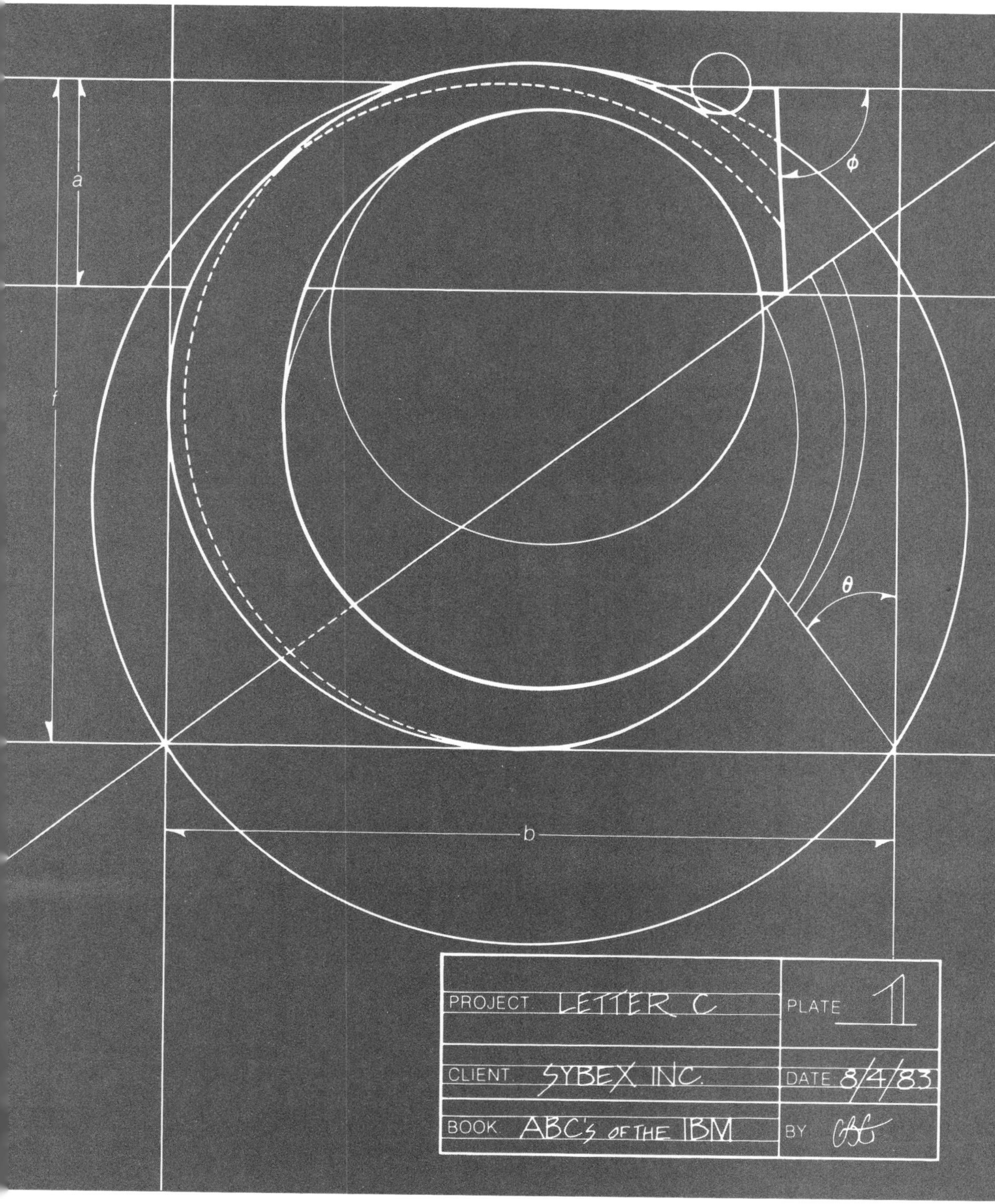

a
f
b
ϕ
θ
PROJECT LETTER C
PLATE 1
CLIENT SYBEX INC.
DATE 8/4/83
BOOK ABC's OF THE IBM
BY

TYPING COMMANDS DIRECTLY

Typed commands are words that have special meanings. With them, you instruct your PC to perform specific tasks. Each software application has its own set of commands. However, once you become familiar with different applications, you will see that they have some commands in common.

The typed commands you use with your PC are related to the task you want the software to perform. Sometimes the command name directly reflects the task. For example, LIST, PRINT, and DELETE are common commands that are used with many software applications. However, most of the time the command is expressed in a kind of shorthand. The command DIR, for example, lists all the files in the directory and the command CHKDSK checks the amount of space available on the diskette. Occasionally the commands are not that easy to figure out—EXE2BIN, for example. (Don't worry about what that means for now.)

When you give instructions to people, you often have to give some extra information so that they know exactly what to do. For example, if you give the command *Go,* do you mean *Go to the store* or *Go to the movies?* Software commands are the same. You often have to give additional information so the computer will do exactly what you want.

The extra information you give when you enter a command is called a parameter. Each command has its own set of parameters for which you must supply specific values. For example, if you give your computer the command COPY, your computer needs to know *what* you want it to copy. The name of the file you want copied is a parameter of the command, and you would have to supply the file name in order for the command to be carried out.

Another thing about commands—you must enter them exactly as they are shown in the software's reference manual or the computer will not know what you mean. Type a command incorrectly and your PC will be stumped! It will flash a message like *Bad command name* or *File not found* at you and you will have to enter the command again.

That goes for parameters, too—you need to enter them in a precise way. Type them correctly, and enter them in the correct order. If you change the order, the computer will not know how to interpret the command, or will do something that you did not intend it to do.

We're going to try giving commands using the DOS command DIR as an example. The DIR command tells DOS to display a list or directory of all the files stored on a diskette. DOS gives you the file name, the type of file, the size, and the date and time created. For example:

```
COMMAND    COM    4959    5-07-82    12:00p
FORMAT     COM    3816    5-07-82    12:00p
CHKDSK     COM    1720    5-07-82    12:00p
   .        .       .        .          .
   .        .       .        .          .
   .        .       .        .          .
BALL       BAS    2048    5-07-82    12:00p
COMM       BAS    4352    5-07-82    12:00p
                28 File(s)
```

It also tells you the total number of files on the diskette, in this case 28.

Want to give it a try? Follow these steps:

1. If DOS is not already loaded, load it now.

   If the power is off: Insert the DOS diskette in drive A: and close the drive door. Turn on the power and DOS is automatically loaded.

   If the power is already on: Insert the DOS diskette in drive A: and close the drive door. Simultaneously press the Ctrl, Alt, and Del keys to reset the computer and load DOS.

2. Immediately after the DOS prompt A>, type:

   ```
   A>DIR ←
   ```

   and watch what happens. Did the information move up off the screen faster than you could read it? When this happens, you will want to freeze, or stop, the display.

Freezing the Display

The display screen on your IBM Personal Computer is really a window that shows only a portion of the information available to you. As you fill the screen with information it moves up, one line at a time, out of your view. This is called scrolling.

Figure 3.1: The Ctrl and Num Lock Keys

You can stop the display from scrolling out of view by using the Ctrl key with the key marked Num Lock.

Let's try it.

3. Type:

    A>DIR ↵

4. As soon as the display starts to scroll up, hold down the Ctrl key and press the Num Lock key to freeze the display on the screen. Too fast? Go back to step 3 and try again. (You can also hold down the Ctrl key and press S. Is this easier for you?)

5. When you are ready to start the display scrolling again, simply press any key. Now let's try using the DIR command with a parameter (that extra information you can use with commands).

6. You can use a file name as a parameter to display information about one particular file. For example, when you type:

    A>DIR BASIC ↵

    your PC displays the following on your screen:

```
BASIC     COM     11392     5-07-82     12:00p
              1 File(s)
```

Upper- and Lowercase

With PC-DOS (and many other operating systems), it does not matter whether you enter commands in uppercase (capital) letters or lowercase letters.

7. Type the DIR command again, sometimes using the Shift key for uppercase letters and sometimes not. For example:

   A>Dir ↵
   A>DIR ↵
   A>dir ↵

   You will see that the result is the same whether you enter the commands in lowercase or uppercase or a mixture of the two.

The Caps Lock Key

If you want to type in all capitals, you can use the Caps Lock key instead of having to hold down the ⇧ key. The Caps Lock key works only with the letters on your keyboard. You will still be able to type a ; or a / and you will still have to use the ⇧ key to type a % symbol.

The Caps Lock key is like an on/off key—press it once to type all capitals, and press it again to stop typing capitals. The key does not stay down and there is nothing to indicate that you have pressed it, so you just have to remember. Whether you are using DOS commands or other software on your PC, the Caps Lock key works the same way.

Now enter some commands using the Caps Lock key.

8. Press the Caps Lock key and type:

   A>DIR ↵
   A>DIR BASIC ↵

   These commands give the same results as before.

9. When you have finished typing all capitals, press the Caps Lock key again to turn it off.

Figure 3.2: The Ctrl and Break Keys

Cancelling a Command

Suppose you typed DIR BASYC instead of DIR BASIC; how would you cancel the command so that you could enter it correctly?

You can cancel a command before you press ↵ by holding down the Ctrl key and pressing the Break key. The Break key cancels the command completely so long as you have not pressed ↵. The computer will display ^C to tell you the command has been cancelled. You can then go on with whatever you meant to do.

Use the DIR command again to see how cancelling a command works.

10. Type:

    A> DIR (Do not press ↵)

11. To cancel the command, hold down the Ctrl key and press the Break key.

That's enough about typed commands for now. Let's look at another way of telling your PC what to do.

CHOOSING FROM MENUS

Some software lets you perform functions by selecting them from several options displayed on a list called a command menu. A command menu is like a menu in a restaurant. It lists your choices and you select the one you want.

Software menus usually list the options with letters or numbers in front of them. You make your selection by typing the letter or number.

Software designers use menus rather than typed commands because they make the software easier to use. First of all, they eliminate lots of typing. The command or a description of a function is listed on the menu and you only have to type the letter or number that refers to the one you want. This helps people who are not used to using keyboards communicate with their computer.

The second reason designers use menus is that they make it easier for you to decide what you want by giving you a frame of reference. Also you do not have to remember a lot of command formats because the menu reminds you how to give an instruction to your computer.

Want to try your hand with menus? Hang on just a minute while we tell you how to use function keys and then you can give it a try.

USING THE FUNCTION KEYS

Another way you can communicate with your computer is through function keys. As you know, the function keys are the two rows of keys on the left of the keyboard labeled F1 through F10. Many software applications have you use these function keys to communicate with the program, so take a minute to get used to their layout.

When a software application program uses the function keys, it predefines each one of the keys to perform a specific operation. The function each key performs changes from application to application and can even change within a program.

At this point you are probably wondering *But how do I know which key does what when?* A very good question. Most programs that use function keys save you a lot of confusion by displaying the current meaning of the function keys on the screen, so you can tell which key to use.

Your DOS diskette includes a program called SAMPLES which does things like play music and games. We are going to use this program to demonstrate menus and function keys. SAMPLES was written in the BASIC programming language, so you have to begin by telling DOS you want to use BASIC. *But how can I use BASIC,* you ask, *when I don't even know what it is?*

A Bit about BASIC (and Other Programming Languages)

BASIC (Beginner's All-Purpose Symbolic Instruction Code) is a popular, easy-to-learn, easy-to-use, high-level programming language. High-level means that it resembles the language people speak. Other commonly used, high-level programming languages include COBOL (COmmon Business Oriented Language) which, as its name suggests, is widely used in the business world, and Pascal.

A programming language is a collection of instructions that you use to write programs. We do not go into how to write programs in this book. We assume that at least initially you will buy application programs that other people have written for you. For more information about using BASIC with your IBM PC, consult *BASIC Exercises for the IBM Personal Computer* by J.P. Lamoitier, and *Useful BASIC Programs for the IBM PC* by Stanley R. Trost, both published by Sybex.

Now back to our demonstration program. To see how to use menus and function keys, follow these steps:

1. Immediately after the DOS prompt, type:

   A>BASIC ↵

   This displays the following message, which tells you that BASIC is available for you to use (we are not going to actually use it):

   ```
   The IBM Personal Computer Basic
   Version C1.00 Copyright IBM Corp 1981
   62940 Bytes free
   OK

   _
   ```

2. Look at the bottom of the screen:

```
1LIST 2RUN← 3LOAD" 4SAVE" 5CONT← 6,"LPT1 7TRON← 8TROFF← 9KEY 0SCREEN
```

The numbers of the labels on the screen refer to the corresponding function keys on the keyboard. For example, the label 1LIST on the screen corresponds to function key F1 on the keyboard, 2RUN corresponds to function key F2, and so on. You choose a function by pressing the appropriate key. The labels will vary depending on the application program, but the numbers always refer to the same keys.

3. You are ready to load the SAMPLES program, so press function key F3 on the keyboard. This corresponds to the label 3LOAD" and the prompt *LOAD"* will appear at the top of the screen.
4. Now type the name of the program immediately after LOAD":

   LOAD"SAMPLES ↵

5. When the program has been loaded, you will see *Ok* on the screen.
6. To start the program, known as running the program, press function key F2, labeled 2RUN on the screen.
7. You will see the following message:

IBM
Personal Computer

SAMPLES

Version 1.10

(C) Copyright IBM Corp 1981, 1982

Press space bar to continue

Notice the instruction at the bottom of the screen telling you to press the space bar to continue. Your PC will often give instructions at the end of a display, so you should keep an eye on this space.

8. Press the space bar. Your PC displays:

```
        SAMPLE PROGRAMS

    A - MUSIC              (48k)
    B - ART                (32k-Color/Graphics)
    C - MORTGAGE           (48k)
    D - CIRCLE             (BASICA-Color/Graphics)
    E - DONKEY             (BASICA-Color/Graphics)
    F - PIECHART           (BASICA-Color/Graphics)
    G - BALL               (BASICA-Color/Graphics)
    H - COLORBAR           (32k)
    I - CALENDAR           (32k)
    J - SPACE              (BASICA-Color/Graphics)
    ESC KEY - EXIT

    ENTER LETTER OF PROGRAM

    NOTE: All of the above programs
          require 48k if using BASICA
```

   This display is a menu. It lists letters of the alphabet down the left side, with different options next to the letters. You choose one by typing the letter shown next to it. The right-hand column also tells you the things your computer needs to run the options. For example, you cannot choose B, D, E, F, G, and J if you do not have color graphics.

9. Let's have your computer play some music. Type an A and press ↵.
10. Your PC loads the MUSIC program and the display tells you to press the space bar to continue.
11. Another menu appears. Which tune would you like to hear? Type the letter next to its title. For example, type H for *Yankee Doodle* and press ↵ .
12. When you have had enough of all this nonsense, press the Esc key to return to the SAMPLES menu. (We will tell you what Esc does in a minute.)
13. Press Esc again to leave, or exit from, the SAMPLES program.

14. You have stepped out of MUSIC into SAMPLES and out of SAMPLES into BASIC, but you still have to get out of BASIC. To return to the DOS operating system, type:

    SYSTEM ↵

    and you will be back where you started at the DOS prompt.

The Esc Key

The Esc (escape) key may perform different functions in different application programs, but basically it is used to get you out of situations you don't want to be in. For example, it got us out of MUSIC and back to the SAMPLES program. It is also used to interrupt programs or commands. Some programs will ask you to confirm that you really want to interrupt the process; others will assume that you know what you are doing. Check the program documentation to find out exactly how the Esc key works for that program.

REVIEW

Three ways to tell your PC what to do :

- Type a command (a precise word or group of words).
- Choose a menu option by typing its letter or number.
- Choose one of the function keys (F1 through F10 on the keyboard) that corresponds to a screen label.

Figure 3.3: The Esc Key

Use the DIR command to:

- List all files on the diskette.
- List a single file when you include the file name with the command.

To stop the display from scrolling out of view:

- Hold down Ctrl and press Num Lock to freeze the display.
- Press any key to start it again.

To type in capitals:

- The Shift key (⇧) gives an uppercase letter or a symbol from the top row.
- The Caps Lock key gives all capitals; press it once for all capitals, press it again to end capitals.

To cancel a command:

- Hold down Ctrl and press Break.

four

All About Diskettes

All the information you need to make your computer work for you is stored on diskettes. Without diskettes, your PC is useless. Diskettes don't look that important, do they? But don't be fooled—appearances are deceiving.

Diskettes are also known as floppy diskettes or floppies. They are called floppy because they bend easily. For this reason they have a protective covering that keeps them flat. The actual diskette on which the information is stored spins inside this cover. Information is read from and written to the PC's memory by a read-write head (similar to the playing arm on a record player) from the cut out area on the diskette.

Diskettes come in three sizes, the standard 8-inch, $5\frac{1}{4}$-inch, and most recently, 3-inch. The diskettes you use match the size of your diskette drives; for the IBM PC, they are $5\frac{1}{4}$-inch.

θ
φ
r
f
e
d
a
b
c
PROJECT: LETTER A
PLATE 1
CLIENT: SYBEX INC.
DATE: 8/4/83
BOOK: ABC's OF THE IBM
BY

It is not important that you understand how information is stored on a diskette; however, a couple of points can help you out on your first trip to your computer store. First, information can be stored on one or both sides of a diskette. Diskettes that use only one side are called single-sided and those that use both sides are called double-sided. Most PC's used double-sided diskettes; however, your diskette drives may be single-sided. Second, the amount of information you can store on a diskette can vary. Some diskettes are single-density; others are double-density. Double-density simply means the diskette is able to store twice as many characters as magnetic impulses in the same amount of space as a single-density diskette.

In this chapter, we will talk about how to handle, label, store, and copy your diskettes, but first of all, here are a few general rules to follow. These are the DON'Ts. They are here at the beginning so they are sure to catch your attention.

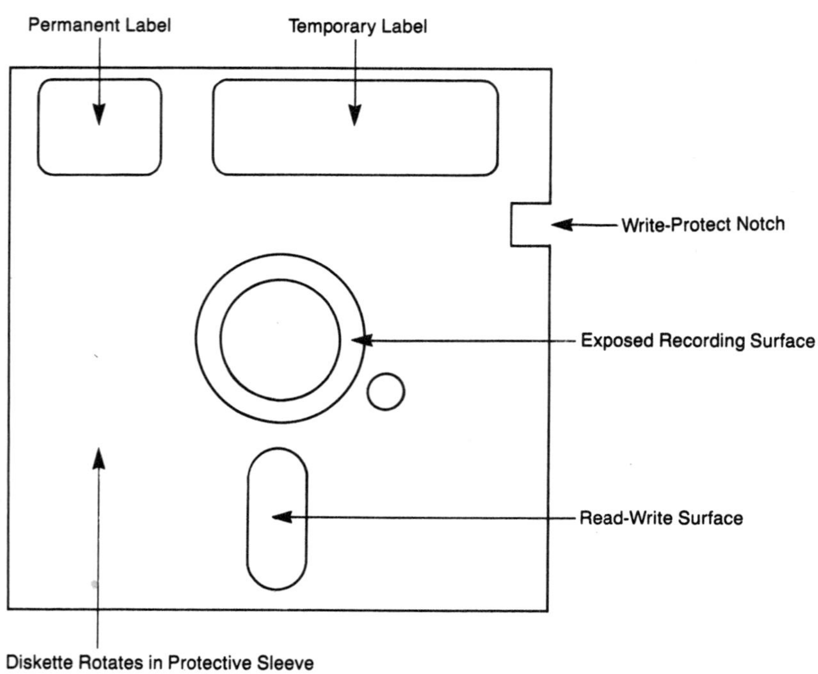

Figure 4.1: A Diskette

- DON'T touch the exposed surfaces of a diskette.
- DON'T bend or fold a diskette.
- DON'T write on diskette labels with a sharp pencil or ball point pen.
- DON'T put diskettes near magnetized objects.
- DON'T put them in places that are very hot or very cold.
- DON'T let your diskettes get dusty.
- DON'T put diskettes near liquids and chemicals that may give off vapors.

What is the reason for all these DON'Ts? Diskettes are like record albums—you can record information on them and also play it back. Recording information is known as writing to the diskette; playing it back is known as reading the diskette. All of the things listed above can mar the surface of the diskette in such a way that your PC can no longer write or read information. A little carelessness and valuable information might be totally lost! Take time to familiarize yourself with the DON'Ts now and save yourself a lot of aggravation later on.

Now we can talk about the DOs.

LABELING DISKETTES

You will probably want to save related information on the same diskette, so that you can label each diskette with a general title. For example, if the diskette contains all the reports for one sales region, an appropriate label is Western Sales Region. When pertinent, you might also include the date. Just as a book does not give all its chapter titles on the cover, don't try to keep all the file names on the diskette label—the main subject is all you need. You can always get a complete file listing using the DIR command.

Diskette manufacturers provide sticky labels with each box of diskettes that you buy. Use them. Write the title on the label before you stick it on the diskette. If you want to change the title or write on the label after you have attached it to the diskette, use a felt tip pen *only*. Ball-point pen and pencil are out—they can damage the diskette surface and make it unusable.

Place the diskette label in the upper right corner of the diskette next to the manufacturer's label. The labels are then all in one place for easy reference and storage. Be sure you do not put the label over any of the exposed surfaces—if you do, your PC will not be able to read from or write to the diskette.

STORING DISKETTES

Store your diskettes in a safe, easily accessible place. As the number of applications that you use and the amount of information you have stored on diskettes increase, storage becomes more and more of a concern.

Many manufacturers package software the same way IBM does, in a plastic sleeve that fits in the back of the application reference binder. You can store the software diskette there, or you may want to keep all of your applications together in a storage container. Several different kinds of diskette containers are available at computer stores or through other hardware and software vendors. Most offer some kind of filing divider and dust cover.

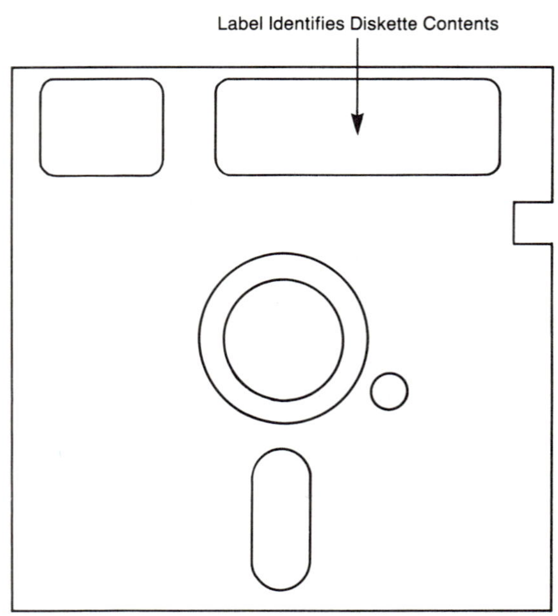

Figure 4.2: Labeling a Diskette

If you don't have a special diskette file, you can use the box you get when you buy diskettes. No matter how you store them, remember to use the paper sleeve they are delivered in. This protects them from dust and prevents you from accidentally touching the surface of the diskette.

Diskettes that contain highly sensitive or irreplaceable data should be stored even more carefully—under lock and key if necessary. Treat your computer software and stored documents just as you would any valuable document. In fact, go one step further and make a copy of your diskettes.

COPYING DISKETTES

What if your computer malfunctions, or you delete something by mistake, or you simply lose a diskette? Things can go wrong, and they will. So get into the habit of backing up your software and information files.

Backing up means making a copy of the information stored on diskette. It protects you from losing information. You cannot appreciate the importance of adequate backup until you don't do it and wish you had. Most people don't bother at first, but, sooner or later, they lose an important file. From that point on, they are always careful to make backup copies.

You can make a copy of everything on a diskette or of a single file. Right now, we are going to talk about copying the entire diskette, the procedure most useful for copying software programs. For example, you will want to make a copy of DOS.

The manufacturers of some application software, such as the VisiCalc program, copy-protect their diskettes, which prevents you from copying them. However, you should always check your purchased software and make a backup copy if you can.

The DISKCOPY Command

Make a copy of the information on a diskette with the DISKCOPY command, which is part of DOS. You will need two diskettes: the diskette containing the information you want to copy, known to DOS as the source diskette; and a blank diskette, known to DOS as the target diskette, onto which the information will be copied.

With the DISKCOPY command, you identify the diskettes by the drives into which they are inserted. On a two-drive system, A: is the left drive and B: is the right one. You can copy all the information from the diskette in A: to the one in B: or *vice versa.* On a single-drive system, you have only drive A:. How you use the DISKCOPY command with a single-drive system is explained in *Appendix B.*

Since you will want to copy the DOS diskette right away, follow these steps to see how DISKCOPY works:

1. Insert the DOS diskette in drive A: and load it if you have not already done so.
2. Insert a blank diskette in drive B: and close the drive door.
3. To copy the DOS diskette in drive A: onto the blank diskette in drive B:, type:

   A>DISKCOPY A: B: ↵

   You are telling your PC to copy *from* the diskette in drive A: *to* the diskette in drive B:. The order is very important. If you wanted to copy from the diskette in drive B: to the diskette in drive A:, you would type DISKCOPY B: A: and press ↵.
4. Your PC displays the message:

   Insert source diskette in drive A::
   Insert target diskette in drive B::
   Strike any key when ready

   Since you have already inserted the diskettes, press any key to begin the copy operation.
5. The red lights on the diskette drives go on and you hear a whirring sound and the message *Copying 1 side(s)* is displayed. When the diskette has been copied, you are asked:

   Copy another (Y/N)?

6. You do not want to copy another diskette so type *N* (for no).
7. Remove the DOS diskette from drive A:, return it to its protective sleeve, and store it in a safe place. From now on, use the backup copy as your everyday, working copy of DOS.
8. Remove the backup copy of DOS from drive B:. Before you put it away, take time to label it. Write *Backup Copy of DOS*

on a label and add the version number that is on the original DOS diskette (probably 1.1 or 2.0). Peel off the label and place it in the top right corner of the diskette.

Before we go on, one word of caution about the DISKCOPY command. Don't use it to copy onto diskettes that already contain information. DISKCOPY starts at the beginning of the diskette and copies until it finishes. If files already exist on the diskette, DISKCOPY writes over them. This is called—guess what—overwriting! Sometimes you want to overwrite, but often you don't. So make it a habit to always DISKCOPY to an empty diskette unless you have a good reason for doing otherwise.

WRITE-PROTECTING DISKETTES

You need to be able to read all your diskettes, but you may not want to be able to write on some. For example, you probably will not want to write on application-program diskettes such as VisiCalc or WordStar. If you accidentally copy over or delete some of the program files, the application simply will not work. You will want to protect these and other diskettes from being changed, either by yourself or others, by using a write-protect tab that prevents information from being added to or deleted from the diskette.

Like labels, write-protect tabs are provided with diskettes when you buy them. They are small foil stickers that you place over the square notch on the side of the diskette. They are removable so if you put a tab on a diskette to protect information that you do not want changed today, and tomorrow you decide that you want to change the information or overwrite the diskette, you can always take it off again.

Take a moment now to write-protect the copy of DOS that you made with the DISKCOPY command:

1. Remove a foil write-protect tab from the sheet of tabs provided with your diskettes.
2. Place the tab over the notch on the diskette as shown in Figure 4.3.

Now you are safe. No information can be added to or deleted from the diskette unless the tab is removed.

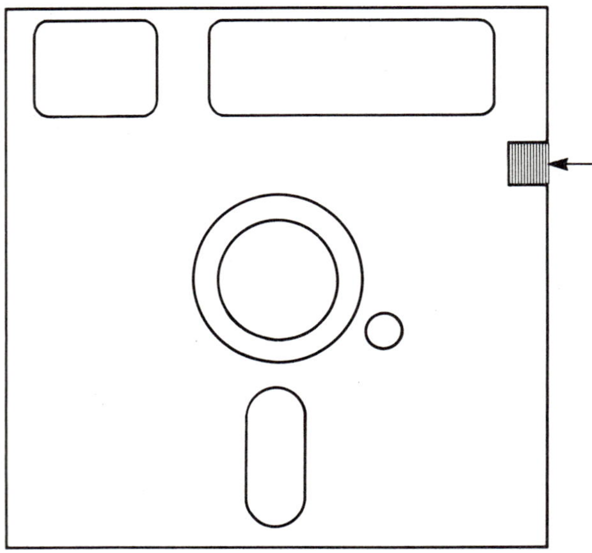

Figure 4.3: Write-Protecting a Diskette

CHECKING DISKETTE STORAGE SPACE

Information is stored on diskettes in bytes. You can think of one byte as the amount of space needed to store one character. It is a little more complicated than that, but that's pretty much all you need to know for now.

The memory of your computer is measured in thousands of bytes (sometimes called kilobytes or K bytes, as in 64K bytes of memory), and so is the storage capacity of diskettes. For example, a double-sided diskette has 320K bytes, the equivalent of 160 double-spaced printed pages. A single-sided diskette has 160K bytes, the equivalent of 80 double-spaced pages.

When you first start working with your PC, you will be tempted to use a separate diskette for everything you do. This is great for diskette manufacturers and dealers, but probably not the most efficient use of your diskettes. You may fall into this habit because you are nervous about running out of diskette space—it is impossible to tell how much information you have stored on a diskette by looking at it. But don't worry; DOS can help you out with the CHKDSK command, which tells you how much diskette space you have used and how much you have left.

The CHKDSK Command

The CHKDSK command can help you manage your diskettes to full advantage. If you want to copy a program or report onto a diskette that already contains some information, you can use CHKDSK to find out if there is enough room.

Use your backup copy of DOS and practice checking diskette space by following these steps:

1. Insert the diskette in drive A:, close the drive door, and reset the computer.

2. Check the status of the diskette, including available space, by typing:

   ```
   A>CHKDSK ↵
   ```

   You will receive a report that looks like this:

   ```
   160256    bytes total disk space
     8704    bytes in 2 hidden files
   148480    bytes in 28 user files
     3072    bytes available on disk

   262144    bytes total memory
   249744    bytes free
   ```

   As you can see, of the 160,256 bytes of storage on the diskette, DOS uses 153,088 (8,704 plus 148,480), leaving 3,072 available for additional information.

   In addition, your computer tells you a bit about itself; of the 262,144 bytes of space in its memory, 12,400 are being used and hence 249,744 bytes are free. Those 12,400 bytes are taken up by DOS—remember, when you load DOS, it is copied from the diskette into memory. If you want to use an application program such as VisiCalc, you have to load that into memory, too. The remaining memory is used as temporary storage for the reports or documents you are using with the application program.

3. It does not matter whether you insert the diskette in drive A: or drive B: as long as you tell DOS where to look for it. To check a diskette in drive B:, type:

   A>CHKDSK B: ↵

   This tells DOS to check the diskette in drive B:. Since we do not have a diskette in drive B:, this message appears on the screen:

   Not ready error reading drive B:
   Abort, Retry, Ignore?_

   If you press *A* for Abort, your PC will abandon the command and display the DOS prompt. If you press *R* for Retry, the same message will be repeated, unless you have inserted a diskette in drive B: in the meantime. If you press *I* for Ignore, you will see *Diskette not initialized,* your PC's way of saying it does not recognize what is in drive B: (hardly surprising!), followed by the DOS prompt. Type CHKDSK B: again and try each of these for yourself.

CLEANING THE DISKETTE DRIVES

Diskette drives should be cleaned on a regular basis depending on the amount of time you use your PC. Keeping the environment as free from dust as possible and cleaning the diskette drives on a regular basis are important maintenance steps.

The easiest way to clean the drives is with purchased cleaning kits which are available, with other computer supplies, at computer dealers. Each kit includes instructions for proper use, and usually either a pretreated fabric diskette or one that you treat with a cleaning solution. (Use only the cleaner provided in the kit.)

Turn on your PC, insert the cleaning diskette into the drive, and close the door. Leave it in for about a minute and then remove it. It's as simple as that!

Here is a quick review of this chapter; then we will tell you something about files.

REVIEW

Four things about diskettes:

- Used to store information.
- Can be written to and read from.
- Can be write-protected by covering the write notch with a special tab.
- Must be handled with care.

Using diskettes:

- Label for easy reference.
- Store in a safe, dust-free spot.
- Back up all information.
- Do not write on the diskette surface.

Copying with the DISKCOPY command:

- Copies all the information from one diskette to another.
- Identifies the diskettes with the drives in which they are inserted.

Checking space with the CHKDSK command:

- Checks the diskette in the designated drive.
- Displays a status report that includes the amount of free space on the diskette and in the PC's memory.

Cleaning the diskette drives:

- Do on a regular basis depending on frequency of use.
- Use a purchased cleaning kit.

five

B

Building a Filing System

All the information you store on diskettes is organized in files. If you think of a diskette as a record album, then files are like the songs or cuts. Just as many cuts can be recorded on one album, many files can be stored on one diskette.

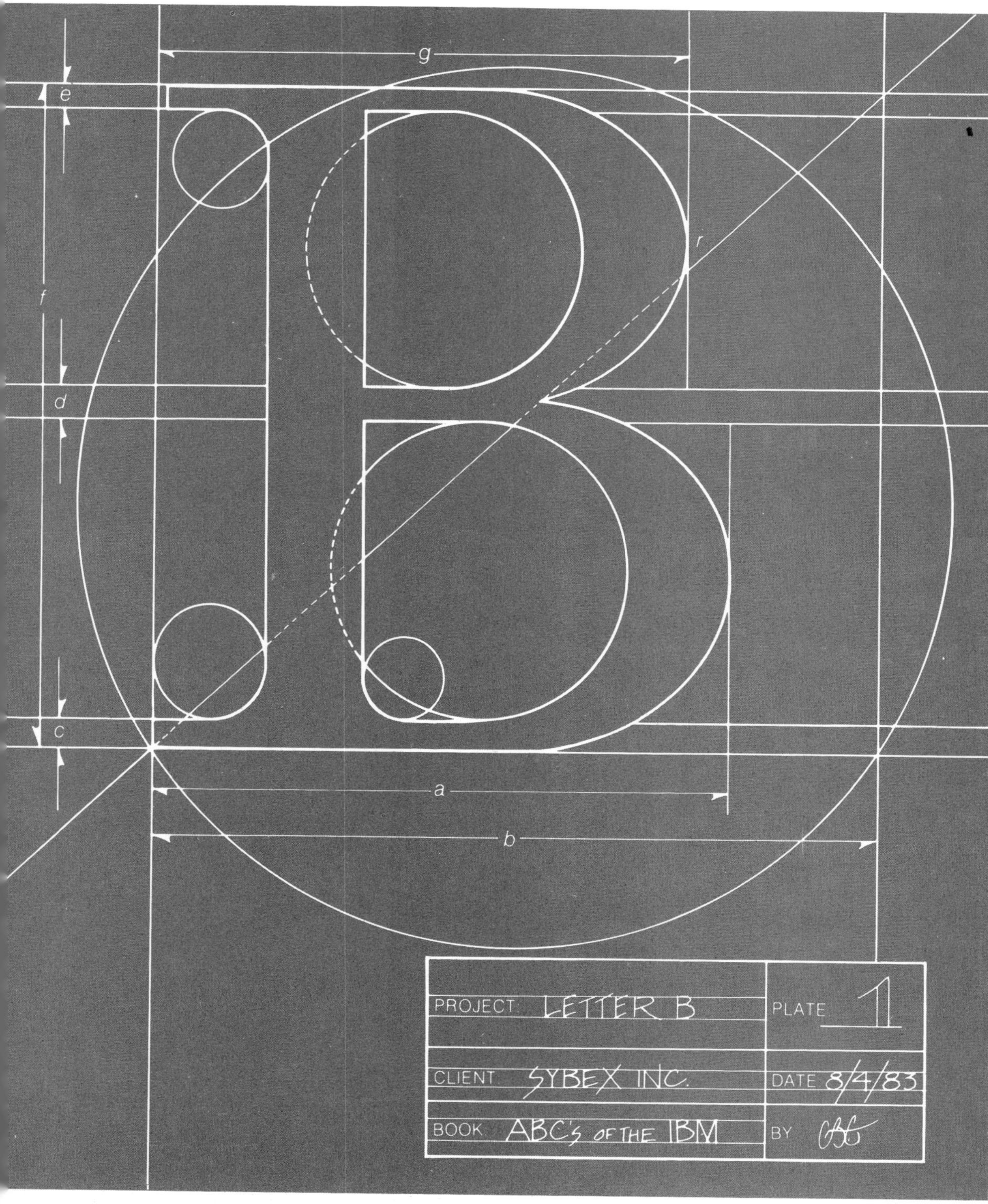

g
e
f
d
c
r
a
b
PROJECT: LETTER B
PLATE 1
CLIENT SYBEX INC.
DATE 8/4/83
BOOK ABC's OF THE IBM
BY

ASSIGNING FILE NAMES

Each file is identified by a unique name. Whenever possible, choose names that reflect the information stored in the file. For example, SALESRPT is a good name for a sales report file, and TESTPLAN is probably the best name anyone could come up with for a file containing a project test plan. What if you forget the exact name of a file? Don't worry—you can always list all the files stored on a diskette with the DIR command.

Rules for File Names

A file name must be between one and eight characters long. It can consist of letters, numbers, or symbols. However, it must begin with a letter and cannot contain a period, an asterisk, a question mark, or a space. If you are using DOS 2.0, you cannot use the following symbols either: < > , :, ;, =, [ ].

Obviously, as you accumulate more and more files, you will find it harder to come up with unique, meaningful file names when you have only eight characters to play with. To overcome this problem you have the option of tagging something called an extension onto the end of the file name. Extensions consist of a period followed by one to three characters. You can use them to identify the type of information in the file. For example, you could use the extension .LET to identify letters, or the extension .DOC for documents. If you give a file name an extension, you must include it any time you refer to the file.

Some application programs, such as the VisiCalc program, use extensions to distinguish different file formats, whereas program files are followed by an extension that identifies the language in which they are written. For example, BASIC program files have the extension .BAS. These extensions are added automatically to the file name when you save the file. You do not have to enter them with the file name.

Here are some file names that obey the rules:

REGION3
SALESRPT.83
VISIDATA
REDINC.LET

These file names do not obey the rules:

1STFILE	(begins with a number)
MAIL LIST	(includes a space)
JONES ACCOUNT	(more than eight characters and includes a space)
MR.SMITH	(includes a period—SMITH is not a valid extension)

When you begin naming files, adopt some kind of system. If most of your work is word processing, you may want to store all documents for a particular account on the same diskette and follow a convention for naming letters, proposals, and project reports. If you frequently do reports with VisiCalc, you might want them all on one diskette also, but since the diskette would then include data for many clients, you would want to name the report files so that you could easily identify to which client a particular report belongs.

USING FILE NAMES WITH COMMANDS

You have already used a file name with a command, but you may not have realized that was what you were doing. In *Chapter 3*, you had your PC list the details of a file named BASIC by entering the command DIR BASIC. You can do this with any of the files on your diskettes. All you do is give the command, the file name, and the extension if there is one.

You can also precede the file name with either A: or B: (the drive identifier) to tell DOS where to look for the file. You will use drive identifiers a lot if you have two diskette drives on your PC. For example, B:NEWFILE.LET tells DOS to look for the file named NEWFILE.LET on the diskette in drive B:. When giving a command, be sure to include : as part of the identifier; for example, DIR B:NEWFILE *not* DIR B NEWFILE.

If you do not include the drive identifier, DOS assumes that it will find the file needed on the diskette in the current drive. Just to remind you, the current drive (also called the default drive or the logged drive) is indicated by the DOS prompt. When the prompt is A>, you know the current drive is drive A:; when it is B>, you know the current drive is drive B:.

If you request a file without the identifier and the file is not in the current drive, you receive the message:

```
File not found
```

All you need to do is retype the file name preceded by the drive identifier.

Wild Card Characters

In a card game, a wild card can represent any card in the deck. DOS has two wild cards, the asterisk * and the question mark ?. An * in a file name or extension means that any character can fill that position and any remaining positions in the name or extension. A ? in a file name or extension means that any character can fill that position only.

Once you start to build a library of diskettes, each containing many files, you will find wild card characters an easy way to work with groups of file names. For example, you can list a group of files, perhaps all files beginning with M, or all files with the extension .BAS.

Here's how wild card characters work.

1. Use the copy of DOS that you made in *Chapter 4*. Remove the write-protect tab. Later on in this chapter we are going to be adding information to the diskette—your PC will refuse to do this if the write-protect tab is still in place.
2. Insert the DOS diskette in drive A: and load it.
3. Use * to list all files beginning with M. Immediately after A>, type:

   ```
   A>DIR M*↵
   ```

   Your PC lists the three files on the DOS diskette that begin with M.

   ```
   MODE        COM    2509    5-07-82    12:00p
   MORTGAGE    COM    6272    5-07-82    12:00p
   MUSIC       BAS    8704    5-07-82    12:00p
                   3 File(s)
   ```

4. To list all files with the extension .BAS, type:

   A>DIR *.BAS ↵

   If your copy of DOS is the same as ours, this command lists 12 files, all with the extension .BAS.

5. Try using a ? to list all files that are named BASIC or BASIC followed by another character. Type:

   A>DIR BASIC? ↵

   Two file names are listed on our copy of DOS.

   ```
   BASIC     COM
   BASICA    COM
   ```

   If there were a file named BASICAL on the DOS diskette, it would not be listed with the ?—you would have to use *.

COPYING FILES

You have already used the DISKCOPY command to copy an entire diskette. Often you will want to copy only a single file or group of files, not the whole diskette. That is what the COPY command is for.

Making a Copy on the Same Diskette

When you copy a file, you do just that—copy it. It is like using your office copier. The original remains intact, but you now have a duplicate. Why would you want to copy a file? Well, for example, suppose you produce a monthly report. Instead of redoing the whole thing each month, you would simply make a copy of last month's report, update the copy in a few places, and store it as this month's report. If you used the original rather than a copy, you would no longer have a report for last month!

When you copy a file from one place on a diskette to another, you must give the copy a different file name—DOS will not allow you to have more than one file with the same name on one diskette. So, for example, the copy of a file named SALESRPT might be called SALESRPT.CPY.

If you want to copy a file on the diskette in the current drive, you do not need to give the drive identifier. You simply give the name of the original file, followed by a space and the name of the duplicate file. (We will tell you later how to copy files from the diskette in the current drive to a diskette in the other drive and *vice versa*.)

Let's try making a copy of the file ART.BAS on your DOS diskette (the backup copy, remember!). We will call the copy DRAW.

1. Type:

   A>COPY ART.BAS DRAW ↵

   Your PC lets you know that it made the copy by returning the message:

   1 File(s) copied

   If you need proof that your PC did as you asked, check the directory by typing:

   A>DIR ↵

   There should now be a file named DRAW at the end of the list.

Remember, when giving a command, include the extension of the file name if there is one and, where appropriate, the drive identifier.

Making a Copy on Another Diskette

Why would you want to copy a file from one diskette to another? One reason is to back up your work. Making a copy of a file on a second diskette means you have a duplicate of the file for safety. There are also lots of other reasons. Let's suppose that you keep all the documents related to each of your clients on separate diskettes. You need to write a letter to Mr. Jones, and you remember that last month you wrote a similar letter to Mr. Smith. Instead of typing the letter all over again, you can copy the letter from Mr. Smith's diskette to Mr. Jones' diskette and make whatever changes are necessary, thereby saving yourself a lot of typing.

If Mr. Jones is a brand new client and you are going to use a brand new diskette to store this first document, you will have to format the diskette before you can make a copy of Mr. Smith's letter.

Formatting a diskette

You did not need to format the diskette when you used the DISKCOPY command because your computer automatically formats the new diskette as part of that command. However, if you are using the COPY command with a new diskette, you will have to use the FORMAT command first.

When you format a diskette, you set the diskette to the recording format for DOS. Back to our stereo analogy again. If a record album has been recorded at 33 rpm and you play it back at 45 rpm, it sounds funny. Diskettes are somewhat the same except that they won't just sound funny; the computer won't be able to work with them at all. If the diskette has not been set to the format for DOS, you cannot even record information on it, let alone read it back.

Each operating system records information in its own format. When you format a diskette, you are indicating which format you are using. This means you do not have to buy different diskettes for different computers—you simply reformat and recycle them.

Formatting performs several operations: it sets the diskette to the correct recording format; checks the diskette for any defective areas that cannot receive information; and prepares the diskette to receive files. The result of all this activity is a diskette that you can use to store information.

To format a diskette, use the FORMAT command followed by the drive identifier of the drive in which the new diskette is inserted. Take time to try it out now. As usual, this example is for a two-drive PC.

1. Insert your copy of DOS in drive A: and load it, and then insert a blank diskette in drive B:. Make sure you use a blank diskette, since the format operation overwrites anything currently on the diskette.

2. Format the diskette in drive B: by typing immediately after A>:

   A>FORMAT B:↵

   Whatever you do, don't forget the B:, or DOS will think you want to format the diskette in drive A: and will wipe out everything on your DOS diskette.

3. Your computer helps you out with this message:

   ```
   Insert new diskette for drive B:
   and strike any key when ready
   ```

   Since you have already inserted the blank diskette, press any key to begin the formatting operation.

4. To let you know things are proceeding as planned, DOS sends you the message:

   ```
   Formatting . . .
   ```

   And, when the operation is complete, it lets you know that too:

   ```
   Formatting...format complete
     322560 bytes total disk space
     322560 total bytes available on disk
   Format another (Y/N)?
   ```

5. At this point you can remove the diskette from drive B:, insert another, type *Y* and continue formatting, or you can simply type *N*.

Once the diskette has been formatted, you are ready to copy a file. When you are copying from one diskette to another, you can use the same name for both versions of the file, unless, of course, you already have a file with that name on the diskette you are copying to.

We will assume you still have DOS loaded and your formatted blank diskette inserted in drive B:. We are going to copy the file SPACE.BAS from the copy of DOS inserted in drive A: to a file also called SPACE.BAS on the diskette in B:.

1. Immediately after A>, type:

   ```
   A>COPY SPACE.BAS B:↵
   ```

   You do not have to include a drive identifier for the original file because DOS will know to look for it on the diskette in the current drive, and since you are using the same file name, you do not need to give a name for the copy you are writing to the diskette in drive B:.

When it has finished the copying operation, DOS gives you the message:

```
1 File(s) copied
```

2. Now let's copy SPACE.BAS from DOS in drive A: to a file we will call ASTRO on the diskette in drive B:. Immediately after A>, type:

```
A>COPY SPACE.BAS B:ASTRO ←┘
```

Again, no need for a drive identifier for the original file, but since you want the copy on the diskette in drive B: to have a new name, you have to tell DOS what the new name will be. When copying is complete, you will see the same message as before on your screen.

3. Want to try an example with wild card characters? To copy all files beginning with the letter E from the diskette in drive A: to the diskette in drive B:, type:

```
A>COPY E*.* B: ←┘
```

Something new happens here. When you use wild cards, DOS lists the name of each file as it copies them so that you know what you are getting. At the end of the copy operation the message on your screen looks like this:

```
EXE2BIN.EXE
EDLIN.COM
2 File(s) copied
```

When you use the * wild card in this way, you need to type an * for the file extension as well as the file name. Typing COPY E* would not have copied any files, since both files beginning with E on the DOS diskette have an extension. Remember, when a file has an extension, you must use it whenever you use the file name.

RENAMING A FILE

What if you think of a better name for a file, or want to change the name to be consistent with other file names? You can always change the name of a file with the RENAME command. You give the current name of the file and the name you want to change it to. It's that simple. The next time you want to look for the file, use its new name. Nothing in the file will change—only the name will be different.

In the previous exercise, we copied SPACE.BAS from the DOS diskette to a diskette in drive B: and called the copy ASTRO. Now we have decided that the name ASTRO is a little too *far out* for us and that the more conservative NEWSPACE would suit us better. Let's rename the file.

1. Immediately after A>, type:

   A>RENAME B:ASTRO NEWSPACE ↵

2. PC-DOS does not give you any message to confirm the change, but you can check that things went smoothly with the DIR command. Type:

   A>DIR B: ↵

There should now be a file called NEWSPACE on the diskette in drive B:. If ASTRO had been on the diskette in drive A:, you would not have had to include the drive identifier.

ERASING OR DELETING A FILE

If you no longer need a file, you can delete it with either the ERASE command or the DEL command. Both do the same thing. The important thing to remember with these commands is that once a file has been deleted, it is gone—there is no getting it back. So be sure you know what the file contains before you delete it.

All you do to delete a file is give the command followed by the file name. As always, the file name includes the drive identifier and extension when they apply.

1. Let's delete the file NEWSPACE on the diskette inserted in drive B:. Immediately after A>, type:

   A>DEL B:NEWSPACE ↵

2. Use the DIR command to check that it has been deleted.
3. Earlier on we made a second copy of the file named ART.BAS on the DOS diskette in drive A:, calling it DRAW. Let's erase

that file now. Immediately after A>, type:

A>ERASE DRAW ↵

Since drive A: is the current drive we do not need the drive identifier.

4. Are you ready to use the wild card character * to delete a couple of files at once? If you remember, we still have copies of the DOS files EXE2BIN.EXE and EDLIN.COM on the diskette in drive B:. Delete them by typing immediately after A>:

   A>DEL B:E*.* ↵

   Be very careful when using * to erase files. You do not want to lose more than you planned on. You could in fact delete all the files on a diskette by typing the ERASE or DEL command with *.*. In response, DOS would give you the opportunity for second thoughts by asking: *Are you sure (Y/N)?* If you know what you are doing, type Y; if not, you can cancel the operation by typing N. Isn't it nice to know DOS doesn't trust you as much as you trust yourself?

At this point, remove the DOS diskette from drive A: and replace the write-protect tab. If you have made an error and lost some of your DOS files, you may have to make another copy. Go back to *Chapter 4* for instructions.

In this chapter, we have covered a lot of information that you will use on a regular basis. So here is a quick review to refer back to as you begin using your PC on your own.

REVIEW

File names:

- Each file on the same diskette must have a unique name.
- A file name can be one to eight characters long and must begin with a letter.
- You cannot include a period, space, asterisk, or question mark in a file name.

File extensions:

- A file extension is a three-character identifier separated from the file name by a period. (It can be less than three characters, but not more.)
- If a file name has an extension, you must include the extension when using the file name.

Drive identifiers:

- The left drive identifier is A: and the right drive identifier is B:.
- To use files on a diskette that is not in the current drive, you must include the drive identifier as a prefix to the file name.

Wild card characters:

- An asterisk in a file name or extension means that any character can fill that position and any remaining positions in the name.
- A question mark in a file name or extension means that any single character can fill that position only.

The COPY command:

- Is used to make a copy of a file:
  - on the same diskette.
  - on another diskette with the same name.
  - on another diskette with a different name.
- Wild card characters let you copy several files at once.

The RENAME command:

- Is used to rename a file.

The DEL or ERASE command:

- Is used to delete a file.

six

Computer Applications: Tools for Your PC

So I know about diskettes and files and DOS commands and menus and function keys, you are saying. *What happens now?* Well, this is the moment you've been waiting for! We are going to talk about application programs, the tools that put your computer to work for you.

Application programs take personal computers out of the domain of the technical expert and turn them into useful and productive tools for everyone. The majority of people use their PCs with application programs selected to meet their particular needs. So this chapter introduces you to applications. You will see that all our rules about diskettes and files are for good reason. Any application you use relies on diskettes to store your information and file names to identify the information you want to work with.

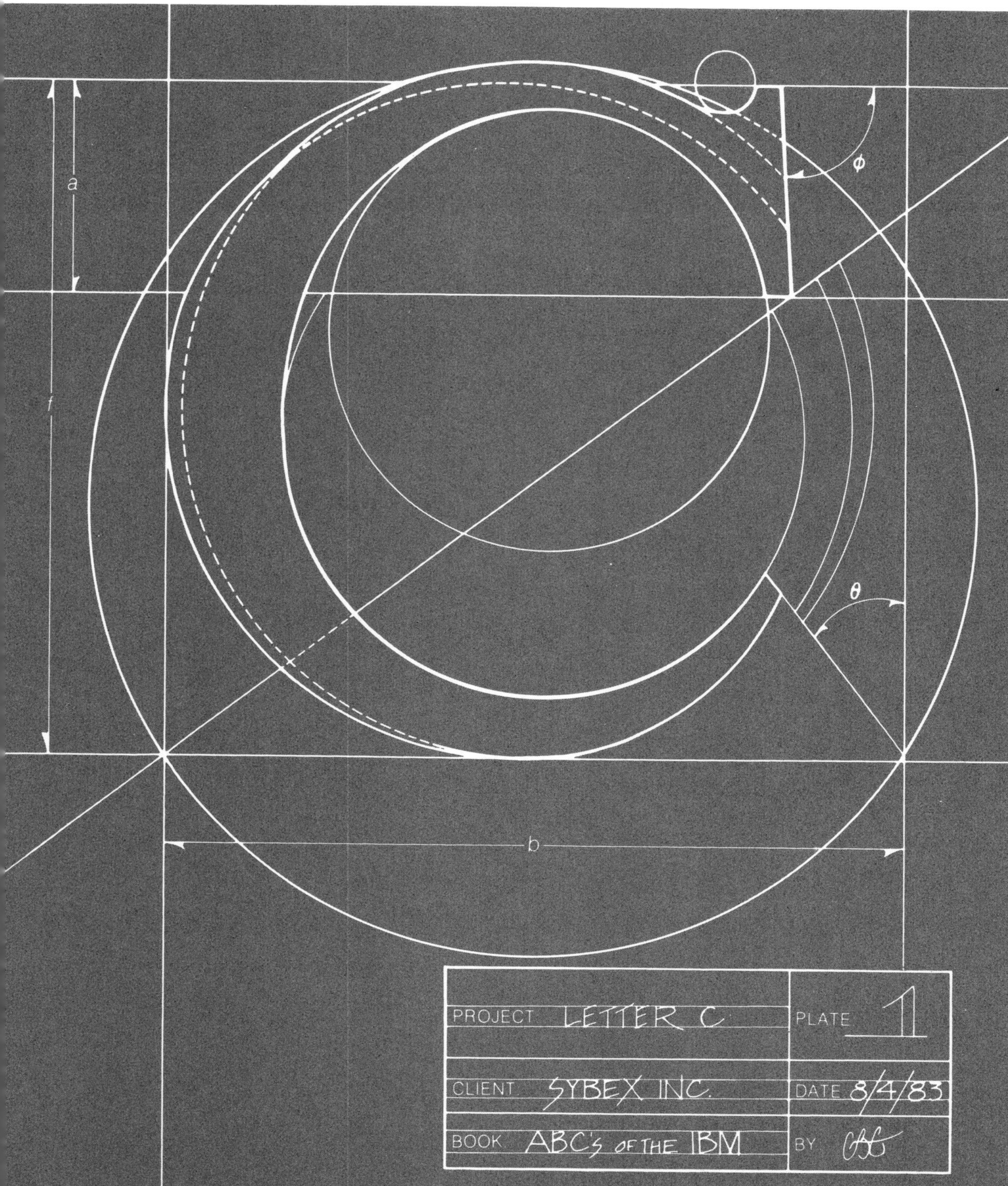

a
f
b
φ
θ
PROJECT LETTER C
PLATE 1
CLIENT SYBEX INC.
DATE 8/4/83
BOOK ABC's OF THE IBM
BY

In Chapter 7, we will show you what it is like to use a couple of applications. We have chosen the most commonly used application programs, word processing and spreadsheets, and introduce you to both without getting you into complicated details. But first, a few basics . . . .

MAKING A BACKUP COPY

As we said in Chapter 4, it is good practice to make a backup copy of your important diskettes. This is just as true for application program diskettes as it is for DOS and your information files. Once you have made a copy of the application, you should store the original diskette in a safe place and use the copy for day-to-day use. If anything ever happens to the copy, you can always make another from the original.

However, like every rule, there are exceptions to this since some application program diskettes are copy protected. This means that the manufacturer has made the diskette in a special way that prevents it from being copied. They usually label these diskettes *Copy Protected* so you will know whether you can copy them or not. In short, if you can copy your application program diskette, you should do so.

1. Load DOS from drive A: as usual.
2. At the DOS A> prompt, type:

   ```
   A>DISKCOPY A: B: ←
   ```

   This displays the message:

   ```
   Insert source target in drive A:
   Insert target diskette in drive B:
   Strike any key when ready
   ```

3. Remove the DOS diskette and insert the application program diskette in drive A:. Insert a blank diskette in drive B:.
4. Press any key to copy the application diskette in drive A: to the blank diskette in drive B:.
5. Remove the application diskette from drive A: and store it in a safe place.

6. Remove the copy from drive B:. Write a label that identifies the diskette (for example, *WordStar Backup Copy*) and place it on the diskette. Put a write-protect tab on the diskette.

LOADING AN APPLICATION PROGRAM

There are two steps to loading any application:

1. Insert DOS into drive A: and load it as usual. Loading DOS is almost always the first thing you do when you want to use your PC. Application programs will not work unless DOS is there first.
2. Remove the DOS diskette and insert the application program diskette, or backup copy, in drive A:. Then type the program name (usually an abbreviation) and press ↵ to load the program.

Self-Loading Applications

Many applications allow you to combine loading DOS and loading the application program into one step by copying the relevant parts of DOS and the application program onto a new diskette. The application then becomes self-loading. The application reference manual will tell you if the application can be made self-loading. If it can, follow these steps:

1. Insert DOS into drive A: and load it as usual.
2. Remove but save the foil write-protect tab from the application program diskette (or the backup copy, if you have one), and insert the diskette in drive B:.
3. At the DOS prompt, type:

   ```
   A>SYS B:↵
   ```

   This command copies the operating system files from the DOS diskette to the diskette in drive B:.
4. When the DOS prompt appears again, type:

   ```
   COPY A:COMMAND.COM B:↵
   ```

This copies the DOS command files to the diskette in drive B:.

5. When the copy operation is complete, remove the application diskette from drive B: and replace its write-protect tab.

The application diskette is now self-loading—you can load both DOS and the application program by putting the application diskette in drive A: and turning on the power, or by resetting your computer (Ctrl, Alt, and Del).

USING AN APPLICATION PROGRAM

All application programs are different—they are intended for different purposes and they work in different ways. Nonetheless, you will perform some typical operations, no matter what application you are using. We are going to introduce you to a few of these now.

Depending on your application, you will give commands, choose menu items, or use predefined function keys to perform the operations we will describe. For example, if you want to save a file, you might type the command SAVE in one application, press a function key labeled SAVE in another, or type a number corresponding to the menu choice SAVE in yet another. So our discussion of these operations is necessarily very general. Hopefully, with a few basic concepts in mind you will find it easier to master the applications themselves.

Entering and Saving Information

Often the first thing you'll do when you start using an application is enter the relevant information. It might be text for use with a word processor, financial information for a spreadsheet, or facts and figures for a data base.

Although your information is displayed on the screen, it is only in your computer's memory for as long as you are working with it. If you leave the application program, reset your computer, or turn off the power, your PC's memory will be wiped clean and you will lose all your information permanently. To avoid this happening you have to store, or save, the information on a diskette before you do any of the above things.

When you tell your PC to save some information, it does so by creating a file on the diskette. You give the file a name before you save it so that next time you tell your PC to retrieve that information, it will know which file you are talking about. (Remember, file names must follow the rules discussed in *Chapter 5.*)

DON'T store your information files on the application diskette itself. If the diskette is write protected, you will not be able to do this anyway. If it is not, storing more information might interfere with the program files.

Instead, use a separate diskette when you are ready to save a file. If it is a new diskette, remember to format it with the FORMAT command before you use it to store information.

Retrieving the Information

Having saved a file, if you want to make changes or just check some information, you will have to load the file from diskette back into the PC's memory first. To do this, you insert the diskette that contains the file in a drive, give the command to read a file, and when the computer asks which file, type its name. Include the drive identifier (A: or B:) as a prefix if the diskette is not in the current drive. If you forget the name of the file, use the DIR command to check the file names on the diskette where the file is stored.

Revising the Information

Once you have loaded the file, you can insert or delete text with your word processor, change the numbers in a spreadsheet report, or add some information to your data base (not all at once of course!).

Keep in mind that when you loaded the file, you made a *copy* and put it in your PC's memory. The original file is still safely stored on its diskette. The changes you make are *temporarily* in the computer's memory and don't become permanent until you save the new version of the file from memory onto diskette again. There are three things you can do with the new version in your PC's memory:

- Don't save the new version at all—wipe your PC's memory clean and forget the file was ever there. If you do not like the changes you have made, or if you just looked at the information but did not change it, there is no harm done. The original version is still on diskette just as if you had never touched it.

- Replace the original version with the new version. If you want to overwrite the original version with the revised version, give the revised version the same name as the original version and save it on the same diskette.
- Save both versions. If you want to keep both the original version and the revised version, give the revised version a different file name if you are going to save it on the same diskette, or save it on another diskette.

Printing the Information

To get a paper copy, or hard copy, of your document, you will need to print it out. Before you start printing, always make sure your printer is connected, turned on, and has paper in it. Some printers also have an on-line button that you have to press before printing. (When a printer is "on-line," it's ready to accept printing instructions from your PC.)

Depending on the application, you will give a PRINT command, select PRINT from a menu, or press a PRINT function key. Then the program usually asks you to give the file name and supply some other details about how it should print the file.

Now for the work sessions. But first of all, here's a review of application programs in general.

REVIEW

Running an application:

- DOS must be loaded before you can use the application.
- Many application diskettes can be made self-loading.

Using an application:

- Operations are performed with commands that are typed directly, chosen from a menu, or selected using function keys.
- Entering, saving, retrieving, revising, and printing information are operations common to most applications.
- Information is saved as a file on diskette. You need to supply the name of the file in order to work with it.

seven

Application Work Sessions

WORDSTAR WORK SESSION

For some people, the main objective for buying a personal computer is to be able to do word processing. Only later do they begin to explore their PC's many other capabilities.

WordStar is a very powerful word-processing program and it takes a little time to master all its commands, so we will not have time to tell you even half the story here. However, we are going to enter some text and play around with it a little.

If you own another word-processing program rather than WordStar, don't skip over this work session thinking it a waste of your time. Reading through the exercise will give you an idea of how word processors work even though the commands for your program may be different.

θ
φ
r
e
d
f
a
b
c
PROJECT LETTER A
PLATE 1
CLIENT SYBEX INC.
DATE 8/4/83
BOOK ABC's OF THE IBM
BY

If you are interested in learning more about WordStar, consult *Introduction to WordStar* by Arthur Naiman, and *Practical WordStar Uses* by Julie Anne Arca, both published by Sybex.

Before You Begin

Insert a formatted, blank diskette in drive B:. We will use this diskette to save the document you are going to create. Do not save documents on the WordStar program diskette since you run the risk of messing up the program by writing over or deleting essential files.

Make sure the diskette you insert in drive B: is formatted. If it is not, load DOS and use the FORMAT command (FORMAT B:).

If you have only one drive, have a blank, formatted diskette handy and insert it in the drive when you are ready to save your document.

Loading WordStar

1. Load DOS from drive A: as usual.
2. When you see the A> prompt, remove the DOS diskette, replace it with the WordStar program diskette, and close the drive door.
3. At the A> prompt, type:

   A>WS ↵

   to load the WordStar program.

The No-File Menu

The No-File Menu is always displayed on your screen after you load WordStar. *No-file* means that you are not working with a file (also called a document) yet.

You can choose any of the commands listed on this menu by typing the letter shown in front of the command. For example, *DIRECTORY of disk A* underneath the No-File Menu lists the files on the diskette in drive A:. To turn off this listing, type *F* and you will see the *off* and *(ON)* next to the F command change places and the DIRECTORY listing disappear from your screen. Type F again and it will reappear.

```
editing no file
              <<<     N O   F I L E   M E N U     >>>

---Preliminary Commands---    | --File Commands-- | -System Commands-
L  Change logged disk drive   |                   | R  Run a program
F  File directory off (ON)    | P  Print a file   | X  EXIT to system
H  Set help level             |                   |
 ---Commands to Open a file---| E  RENAME a file  | -WordStar Options-
D  Open a document file       | O  COPY a file    | M  Run MailMerge
N  Open a non-document file   | Y  DELETE a file  | S  Run SpellStar   ▲

DIRECTORY of disk A:
```

Figure 7.1: The WordStar No-File Menu

Creating a Document

To show you how WordStar works, we need to create a document that we can play around with. Let's open a file.

1. Type *D*. WordStar displays some helpful information and asks you:

   NAME OF FILE TO EDIT?_

2. Type *B:PRACTICE* and press ↵ to create a file called PRACTICE that will be stored on the diskette in drive B:. In this case, we are opening a new file. However, if we already had a file called PRACTICE on the diskette in drive B:, we would follow these same two steps to tell WordStar to copy the existing file into the computer's memory so that we could work on it.

While WordStar is opening the file, it puts the message *NEW FILE* on your screen. Then you will see the Main Menu, a blank typing area, and the cursor (the blinking underscore that will mark your typing position on the screen when you start entering text).

The Main Menu

Once you have opened a file, a new set of WordStar commands, listed on the Main Menu, is available to you.

```
        A:PRACTICE.DOC    PAGE 1   LINE 1   COL 01              INSERT ON

                         < < <          M A I N   M E N U          > > >

      - -Cursor Movement- -      |   -Delete-  |    -Miscellaneous-      |     -Other   Menus-
^S  char left     ^D  char right | ^G   char   | ^I   Tab      ^B Reform  |     (from Main only)
^A  word left     ^F  word right | DEL  chr lf | ^V   INSERT ON/OFF       | ^J  Help      ^K  Block
^E  line up       ^X  line down  | ^T   word rt| ^L   Find/Replce again   | ^Q  Quick     ^P  Print
          - -Scrolling- -        | ^Y   line   | RETURN End paragraph     | ^O  Onscreen
^Z  line up       ^W line down   |             | ^N   Insert a RETURN     |
^C  screen up     ^R screen down |             | ^U   Stop a command      |
L- - - -!- - - -!- - - -!- - - -!- - - -!- - - -!- - - -!- - - -!- - - -!- - - -!- - - - - - - - -R
▲
```

Figure 7.2: The WordStar Main Menu

In addition to the menu of commands, there are now two other items of interest on your screen.

- **The Status Line** above the words MAIN MENU tells you the name of the document and the cursor position (page, line, and column numbers), and that INSERT is ON, which means that text will be inserted wherever you type it.
- **The Ruler Line** underneath the menu shows your left (L) and right (R) margins and indicates that tabs (!) are set every five spaces. Whatever you type will appear within these margins, and you can use the tab settings by pressing ⇆ .

The remainder of the screen is a blank page for you to type on.

Some WordStar Keys

The command choices on the Main Menu are all preceded with the symbol ^. This symbol is shorthand for the Ctrl key. To choose any of these commands, you have to hold down the Ctrl key and simultaneously type the appropriate letter. This is similar to using the Shift key for a capital letter. For example, if you type a *j*, you get a *j*. Shift and *j* gives you a capital *J*. In WordStar, Ctrl and *j* selects the Help command. (In this work session, our shorthand for this kind of command will be ^J.)

As well as the Ctrl key, you will also use the cursor-movement keys and the Ins (insert) and Del (delete) keys in this work session.

Entering Text

The first thing you will notice when you enter text is that you do not have to press ↵ at the end of a line. WordStar automatically wraps words around to the next line when you reach the right margin.

1. Type the paragraph below to practice entering text. Don't worry about typing mistakes at this point. If you are compelled to correct an error, press the Del key once to delete each wrong letter and retype correctly.

   Entering text with WordStar is just like using a typewriter, except that it's much easier. Since words are automatically wrapped around at line endings, you don't have to worry about carriage returns until you get to the end of a paragraph.

2. Now press ↵ twice to end this paragraph and leave a blank line before typing the next paragraph:

   Editing text is the best part of using a word processor. You can go back and make changes to any part of the text with instant results.

Figure 7.3: The Ctrl, Ins, Del, and Cursor-Movement Keys

Positioning the Cursor

When you want to make changes to existing text, you have to start by positioning the cursor at the point of the change.

1. Practice using the arrow keys to move up (↑), down (↓), right (→) and left (←) through the text you just entered.
2. You can also skip a whole word at a time, either forward or backward through your text. Hold down the Ctrl key and type an *F* (^F) to move the cursor to the right one word at a time. In the same way, ^A moves the cursor to the left one word at a time.

Inserting Text

As the status line tells you, INSERT is ON, which means that text is inserted in your document wherever you type it. When you load WordStar, INSERT is automatically ON. Press the Ins key and you will see INSERT ON disappear from the status line, meaning that INSERT is now OFF. Press Ins again and INSERT ON reappears.

1. To insert an extra phrase in the second paragraph, begin by positioning the cursor on the *c* of the word *changes*:

   Editing text is the best part of using a word processor. You can
   go back and make changes to any part of the text with instant
   results.

2. Now type the phrase *all kinds of* (including the space after the last word). The text is inserted and the line is pushed out beyond the right margin.

   Editing text is the best part of using a word processor. You can
   go back and make all kinds of changes to any part of the text with instant
   results.

3. To reform the paragraph so that it fits back inside the left and right margins, press ^B and watch WordStar adjust the line length.

   Editing text is the best part of using a word processor. You can
   go back and make all kinds of changes to any part of the text
   with instant results.

Deleting Text

You can delete text one character at a time, a word at a time, or a line at a time. You can also delete whole blocks of text, but that's getting a bit fancy for this short work session. Let's delete a few characters first.

1. The Del key deletes one character at a time to the left of the cursor, so you must begin by positioning the cursor to the right of the deletion point. Use the arrow keys to move the cursor to the space following the word *using*.

   Entering text with WordStar is just like using_a typewriter, except that it's much easier. Since words are automatically wrapped around at line endings, you don't have to worry about carriage returns until you get to the end of a paragraph.

2. Press Del until the word *using* is deleted (that's six times, including the space before the word).

   Entering text with WordStar is just like a typewriter, except that it's much easier. Since words are automatically wrapped around at line endings, you don't have to worry about carriage returns until you get to the end of a paragraph.

You can also delete characters to the right of the cursor. Press ^G once for each character you want to delete.

Of course, it would have been easier to delete the word *using* all at once. Let's try this out on a word in the second paragraph.

1. Position the cursor on the *u* of the word *using*.

   Editing text is the best part of using a word processor. You can go back and make all kinds of changes to any part of the text with instant results.

2. Press ^T to delete the entire word.

   Editing text is the best part of a word processor. You can go back and make all kinds of changes to any part of the text with instant results.

Want to try deleting a whole line? Let's eliminate the line at the end of the first paragraph.

1. Begin by positioning the cursor anywhere in the line to be deleted.

   Entering text with WordStar is just like a typewriter,
   except that it's much easier. Since words are automatically
   wrapped around at line endings, you don't have to worry about
   carriage returns until you get to the end of a paragraph.

2. Press ^Y to delete the line.

   Entering text with WordStar is just like a typewriter,
   except that it's much easier. Since words are automatically
   wrapped around at line endings, you don't have to worry about

Typing Over Text

You will sometimes want to go back and type over existing text without inserting. To do this you have to turn INSERT OFF with the Ins key.

1. First, position the cursor on the first letter of the word you want to type over, in this case the *r* of the word *results* in the second paragraph.

   Editing text is the best part of a word processor. You can
   go back and make all kinds of changes to any part of the text
   with instant results.

2. Press the Ins key to turn INSERT OFF. (Notice that INSERT ON is no longer displayed in the status line.)
3. Type the new word *success* over the old word *results*.

   Editing text is the best part of a word processor. You can
   go back and make all kinds of changes to any part of the text
   with instant success.

4. Now press Ins to turn INSERT ON again.

Saving the Document

When you have entered your text and made any necessary revisions, you will want to save the document on diskette for future use.

1. Press ^K, which displays WordStar's block menu. This menu displays commands for different kinds of block operations (those you perform on whole blocks of text).
2. You want to save the file but stay in WordStar, so type a *D*. You will see the message *SAVING FILE B:PRACTICE*, which lets you know that the file is saved on the diskette in drive B:. You will then return to the No-File Menu.

Printing the Document

If you have a printer connected to your PC, you can now print the document to see what it looks like on paper. Before you do this, be sure your printer is turned on and that there is paper in it.

1. Type *P* (for Print) to print the document.
2. WordStar will ask:

   Name of file to print?

3. Type:

   Name of file to print?B:PRACTICE ↵

4. We are not going to bother answering the questions on the screen in this work session. Simply press the Esc key and your printer will go to work.

Leaving WordStar

To leave WordStar, check to make sure that the No-File Menu is on the screen, then type *X* to exit to the operating system.

Listing the File

If you want proof that your file is intact, list the directory of files on drive B: by typing:

A> DIR B: ↵

Your document should show up as:

PRACTICE

unless, of course, you called it by a different name.

If you've finished working with WordStar, you should now remove the program diskette, return it to its protective sleeve, and put it away.

VISICALC WORK SESSION

Of all the applications available, spreadsheets are one of the most popular, and VisiCalc is currently the best-seller in the field. Moreover, it is easy to learn! If you have a copy of the VisiCalc program, you can sit down at your PC with this work session and go through the step-by-step instructions to create a simple report.

Although the work session is designed specifically for VisiCalc, all spreadsheets are remarkably similar, and it is worth reading through the work session even if you do not have VisiCalc, to get some idea of how a spreadsheet works. Though the commands given here are specific to VisiCalc, we have tried to make our discussion general enough to apply to any spreadsheet program.

We do not presume that in one short chapter we can tell you all about VisiCalc. We just want to give you the necessary steps to produce a simple report without going into all the whys and wherefores of every step. There are many other sources of information to supplement the exercise you will do here. The reference manual that comes with the program will help a lot and you might also read *Mastering VisiCalc* by Douglas Hergert and *Doing Business with VisiCalc* by Stanley R. Trost, both published by Sybex.

Before You Begin

Insert a blank diskette in drive B: for saving information. If this is a new diskette, use the FORMAT command (FORMAT B:) to format it first.

If you have only one drive, have a blank, formatted diskette handy and insert it in the drive when you are ready to save the report.

Loading VisiCalc

If your VisiCalc diskette is self-loading:

1. Insert the VisiCalc program diskette in drive A: and close the drive door.

2. Turn on the system power. If the power is already on, reset your computer (Ctrl-Alt-Del) to load VisiCalc.

If your VisiCalc diskette is not self-loading:

1. Load DOS from drive A: as usual.
2. When you see the A> prompt, remove the DOS diskette, replace it with the VisiCalc program diskette, and close the drive door.
3. At the A> prompt, type:

   A>VC80 ↵

   to load the VisiCalc program.

The VisiCalc Worksheet

The top, left-hand portion of the VisiCalc worksheet is always displayed on your screen after you load the VisiCalc program. The entire worksheet is too large to fit on the screen all at once—what you see is just a small part of it. However, special commands and the cursor-movement keys allow you to look at any part you want.

The VisiCalc worksheet consists of:

- **Columns**, identified by the letters across the top. There are 63 columns in all, labeled A through BK. Each column is nine characters wide when you begin.
- **Rows**, identified by the numbers down the left side. There are 254 rows.
- **Cells**, which are the intersections of any column and row. Cells are identified by column letter followed by row number; for example, A1.
- **The Cursor**, which appears as a highlighted rectangle and which indicates the cell VisiCalc is looking at. You use the cursor to move around the worksheet and enter information.
- **The Current Cell Indicator**, which tells you the cell the cursor is currently positioned at.
- **The Entry Contents Line**, which displays the entries you type to create a report.

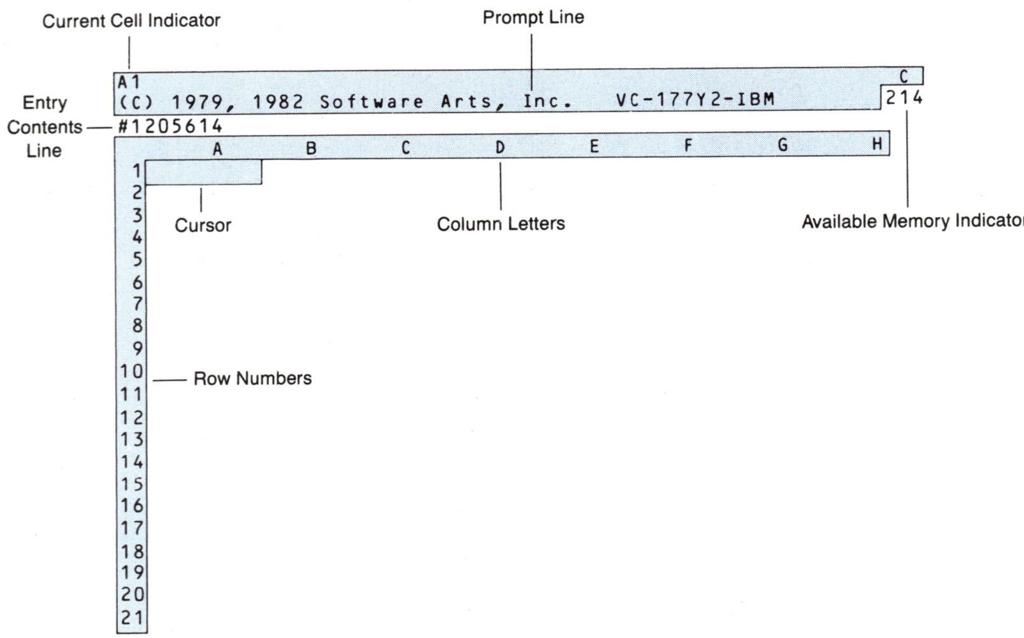

Figure 7.4: The VisiCalc Worksheet

- **The Prompt Line**, which prompts you for information when you use the VisiCalc commands.
- The **Available Memory Indicator**, which tells you how much memory is available in your computer for creating your report.

Creating a Report

When you create a VisiCalc report, you can make three kinds of entry:

- **Labels** are any entry that begins with a letter—they are usually titles for the column or row; for example, Sales, Expenses, Profit.

- **Values** are numbers; for example, 1000, 300, 700.
- **Formulas** perform calculations based on the values you have entered; for example, A2 – B2.

The sample report shown in Figure 7.5 will let you practice making these different kinds of entry.

```
Sales       1000

Expenses     300

Income       700
```

Figure 7.5: Sample VisiCalc Report

There are always three steps involved in making an entry: Position the cursor at the cell that is to contain the entry; type the entry; and enter it on the worksheet.

Figure 7.6 shows some keys you will need to create this report. The arrow keys, as you know, are used to position the cursor. The Slash key (/) displays the VisiCalc commands, and the Greater-than key (>) is used to move the cursor directly to any cell on the worksheet.

Figure 7.6: The Slash, Greater-than, and Arrow Keys

Moving the Cursor

1. Practice using the arrow keys to move the cursor around the worksheet. The → key moves the cursor to the right; the ← key moves it left; and ↑ and ↓ move it up and down.
2. Now you need to move the cursor back to cell A1 to begin creating our sample report. Type > and the prompt line asks:

   Go To Coordinate:

3. Type *A1* and press ↵ to move the cursor directly to cell A1.

Entering Labels

1. To move the cursor to cell A2, press ↓.
2. To enter the label *Sales* in cell A2 and move the cursor down to cell A3, type:

   Sales ↓

3. To enter the label *Expenses* in cell A3 and move the cursor down to cell A4, type:

   Expenses ↓

4. To enter the label *Income* in cell A4, and leave the cursor in this cell, type:

   Income ↵

Entering Values (Numbers)

1. To display *Go To Coordinate:* in the prompt line, type >.
2. To move the cursor directly to cell B2, type:

   B2 ↵

3. To enter the number *1000* (no comma) in cell B2 and move the cursor down to cell B3, type:

   1000 ↓

4. To enter the number *300* in cell B3 and move the cursor down to cell B4, type:

   300 ↓

Entering a Formula

1. To tell VisiCalc you will enter a formula, type a plus sign (+).
2. To subtract Expenses (the number in B3) from Sales (the number in B2), type:

   B2 – B3

3. To perform the calculation and enter the result, 700, in cell B4, press ↵.

And now you know the basics of VisiCalc. Of course, you can do a lot more when you have more experience using it, but you have already mastered creating a simple report.

Saving the Report

The next important step is to save the report on the diskette in drive B: so that you can get it back later. The report will be stored as a file on this diskette, so you have to give it a file name and include the drive identifier as a prefix.

1. To display the VisiCalc commands in the prompt line, type */*.
2. To select the Storage command, type *S*.
3. To select the Save option of the Storage command, type another *S*. VisiCalc displays:

   File for Saving:

4. To call the report INCOME and save it on the diskette in drive B:, type:

   B:INCOME

5. Press ↵ to save the report.

Printing the Report

If you have a printer attached to your PC, you can now print the report. Be sure there is paper in your printer, that it is turned on, and that you have pressed the on-line button if necessary.

1. To display *Go to Coordinate:* in the prompt line, type >.
2. To move the cursor directly to cell A1, type:

   A1 ↵

3. To display the commands, type */*.
4. To select the Print command, type *P*.
5. To select the Printer option of the Print command, type another *P*.
6. Use the ↓ and → keys to move the cursor to cell B4, the last cell used in the report.
7. Press ↵ to print the report.

Leaving VisiCalc

When you are ready to leave the VisiCalc program, you use the Quit option of the Storage command.

1. To display the commands, type */*.
2. To select the Storage command, type *S*.
3. To select the Quit option, type *Q*.
4. To confirm that you want to quit, type *Y* (for Yes).

The VisiCalc worksheet is cleared from the screen and you are back at the DOS A> prompt.

Listing the File

Try listing the directory of files on drive B: by typing:

A> DIR B: ↵

Your report should show up as:

INCOME.VC

The file extension, .VC, tells you this is a VisiCalc file. Since you did not supply another file extension with the file name, VisiCalc went ahead and used its own identifying extension. Remember, if you wanted to make a copy of this file, or delete or rename it, you would have to supply the .VC extension as part of the file name.

REVIEW

WordStar:

- A popular word-processing program.
- Allows you to create a document and enter text.
- Provides automatic word wrap at line endings.
- Lets you go back and easily revise text.
- Inserting, deleting, and typing over text are simple revisions; many other editing and formatting operations are possible.
- Save WordStar documents on diskette if you want to use them later.

VisiCalc:

- A popular financial spreadsheet program.
- A worksheet of columns and rows that intersect to form cells for entering information.
- Cell entries are labels, numbers, or formulas.
- Make an entry by positioning the cursor, typing the information, and entering it on the worksheet.
- Save VisiCalc reports on diskette if you want to use them later.

eight

B

Bells and Whistles: Optional Components

The IBM Personal Computer is different things to different people. To some, it's a sophisticated typewriter—a word processor with a printer attached. To others, it's a fancy calculator that manages their financial affairs. Then there are those who write complex computer programs today and play video games tomorrow. It's a very versatile tool that can be customized for individual use by adding the application programs and bells and whistles that fit your particular needs.

We already told you about adding diskette drives and a display to make a working system. Perhaps the basic PC is all you need, but you don't have to stop there! Add printers and plotters, color and graphics, games and communications—whatever meets your needs or tickles your fancy.

Any of these additional options can be included in your initial PC purchase, or they can be added later as your needs change. The basic system unit has some empty spaces, called expansion slots, to

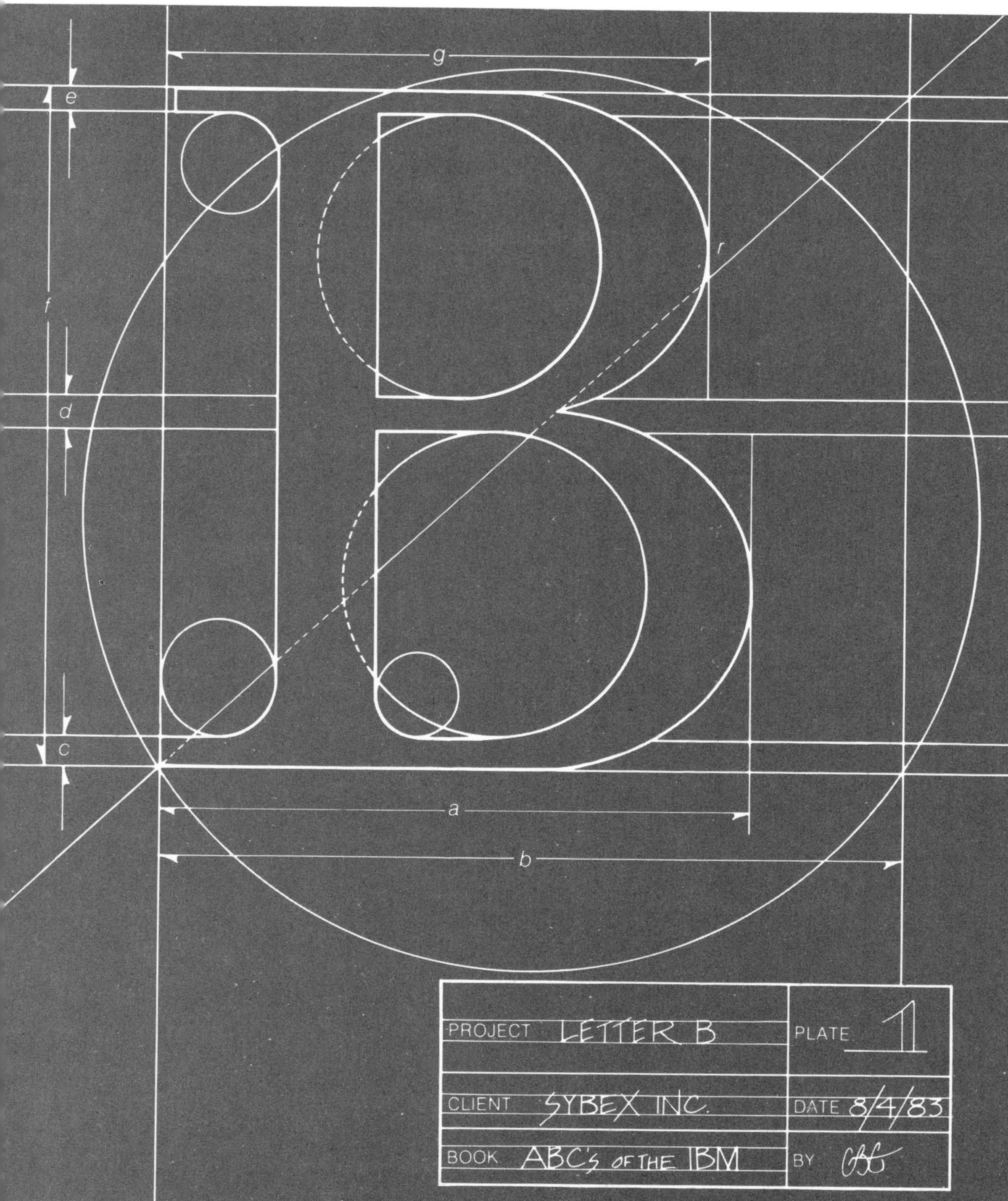

g
e
f
d
c
r
a
b
PROJECT LETTER B
PLATE 1
CLIENT SYBEX INC.
DATE 8/4/83
BOOK ABC's OF THE IBM
BY

accommodate adapters and printed-circuit boards for add-on options. The number of expansion slots is limited, so have someone check the space in your system unit before you purchase an option. Sorry—you can't have everything!

Some options are manufactured and supplied by IBM. Some are specially made by other companies to be compatible with the IBM PC. Since your whole system has to work together, make sure a piece of equipment is compatible with your PC before you rush out to buy it.

This chapter gives you an overview of add-on options for the PC. If you are interested in adding options to your system, the first step is to talk to your IBM dealer to find out what is available. New products are constantly being developed and you will want to know what your choices are before making a purchase.

In addition, be sure you know what else is involved. Do you need special adapters or a specific amount of memory? Do you have to purchase cables and connectors separately? Take some time to check into all this ahead of time and you will be sure to end up with what you wanted.

HARD DISKS

In this book, we have assumed you are using diskettes with your PC, but you can also purchase a hard disk to store information. A hard disk is a large, unbendable version of a diskette, housed in a protective disk unit. In general, you don't remove or insert the hard disk as you would a diskette—it is usually inaccessible and permanently enclosed.

The major advantages of a hard disk are speed, reliability, and capacity. Files can be loaded, revised, and saved more quickly. Hard disks don't wear out and are not as sensitive to the environment and mishandling as diskettes. You can store up to 40 times more information on a hard disk than on a diskette. Of course, all these benefits make a hard disk more costly, a factor to be taken into consideration.

A hard disk can be used to store both your application programs and information files, putting everything you need in one convenient place. If you want to copy files from a diskette to the hard disk, or to keep backup copies of information on diskette, you will also need a diskette drive to transfer the information back and forth.

PRINTERS

For many people, a printer is not an option; it is an essential piece of equipment. If you will be doing word processing or producing any kind of report that needs to be on paper, you will certainly need a printer. Printers come in two flavors, letter quality and dot matrix, so-called because of the kind of print they produce.

Letter-quality print looks as though it comes from an IBM typewriter and is produced in much the same way, with a cartridge ribbon and a print wheel. Like a typewriter element, the print wheel can be changed to produce many different typefaces. This kind of printer is used mostly with word-processing applications or wherever high-quality letters and reports are required.

Dot-matrix print is composed of small dots that give a more uneven appearance than letter-quality print. It's fine for many jobs—program listings, memos, and drafts—but it's not good for more formal business correspondence.

The major deciding factor between the two, then, is the quality of print you require. Other considerations are speed and price. Printer speed is measured in characters per second and varies greatly from printer to printer (anything from 20 to 300 characters per second). In general, dot-matrix printers are faster than letter-quality printers. Another plus for dot-matrix printers is that they are usually less expensive. However, the decision usually comes back to the issue of print quality.

Your printer will come with a printer cable and instructions for connecting it to your PC. For some printers, you may also have to have a special adapter installed in the system unit.

ADDITIONAL MEMORY

The system unit of the PC includes a working memory which temporarily holds the program and information you are currently using. You can have anything from 16 to 512 kilobytes of memory. A kilobyte or K byte is around a thousand bytes, and you can think of a byte as approximately one character, so 16K bytes of memory gives you space for about 16 thousand characters of working information. Your PC may have more memory than this, but it won't have less.

If you work with large programs and information files you will need more memory than if you produce the odd report or memo. More memory increases the PC's ability to handle large jobs, and more is usually better. With word-processing programs, editing a large document goes faster if you have more memory since the whole document can fit in memory at one time. In addition, some application programs and other options specify the minimum amount of memory that your PC must have in order for you to run the program. (Remember the SAMPLES program in *Chapter 3*, where some subprograms required at least 32K bytes of memory and others required at least 48K?)

You buy your PC with as much memory as you think you will initially need. You can have more installed in the system unit later if your needs change.

COLOR/GRAPHICS DISPLAYS

Perhaps you want to produce bar charts, pie charts, and graphs? Or would you like to play video games? With a color/graphics display, you can do both. Graphics and color usually go hand-in-hand; you get color on the screen as well as graphics capabilities.

Although you use a color graphics display primarily for graphics applications, you can also use it with any other application. The quality of text on a color display is not as good as a monochrome display, however, so it does not lend itself well to word-processing applications.

In addition to the color graphics display, you will have to have a color/graphics monitor adapter installed in the system unit. You should also check whether your current version of DOS is compatible. If it is not, you'll need to buy a new version.

GAME CONTROL ADAPTERS

And since we mentioned games, you'll need a game control adapter if you want to play interactive games that use a joystick. IBM doesn't offer game joysticks, but they can be purchased elsewhere and connected to the system unit with the game control adapter.

PLOTTERS

A plotter is like a printer in that it gives you paper output; but there the similarity ends. A printer just prints; a plotter is an electronic artist. Instead of a print wheel, a plotter has colored pens (up to eight) that pick themselves up and move across the paper to write and draw. Plotters are used mainly with graphics applications to produce graphs and charts, as well as overhead transparencies and presentation aids.

To use a plotter with your PC, you will need to have a special adapter installed in the system unit.

COMMUNICATIONS ADAPTERS

Your keyboard and display allow you to communicate with your PC; a communications adapter allows your PC to communicate with other computers.

Computer communications is a wide-ranging area of technology that is constantly developing. It offers many different options. Some require the addition of an acoustic coupler or a modem (electronic, telephone-like devices) and some require that your computer be connected into a communications network, while others require special software programs. What computer communications can offer you will depend entirely on your particular situation, but some possibilites are:

- Sending and receiving electronic mail messages.
- Sending information across telephone lines.
- Sharing information with other PC users.
- Subscribing to public information services (more on these in *Appendix D: Resources*).
- Sharing access to a large central computer.
- Using a printer or disk drive that is not even attached to your PC.

A communications adapter also allows you to use other equipment such as plotters, letter-quality printers, and voice-recognition devices.

nine

C

Checklists: If Something Goes Wrong . . .

And of course it will. Despite the high quality and reliability of the IBM PC itself and the care you take in using it, at some point something will go wrong. When your computer won't do what you want, it can be very frustrating, so this chapter is to give you some pointers for getting out of trouble.

Most problems are caused by one of two things—either you have given the computer incorrect or incomplete instructions, or something really isn't working properly. Hard as it may be to take, the first of these is usually the case. It's worth taking the time to check on yourself before you bundle up your PC and send it off for repair. Even if you are not the culprit, your service person will be able to help you much better if you can be specific about the details of the problem.

Let's start with you. Ask yourself the questions in our *You* Checklist. Does this solve the problem? Don't be embarrassed; we all make these mistakes. Just correct the problem and try again.

If the first list is no help, go on to the *PC* Checklist, which gives some typical trouble areas that you can check for yourself. Although some may sound obvious (*of course* the power is on), you never know who tripped over the power cord when your back was turned.

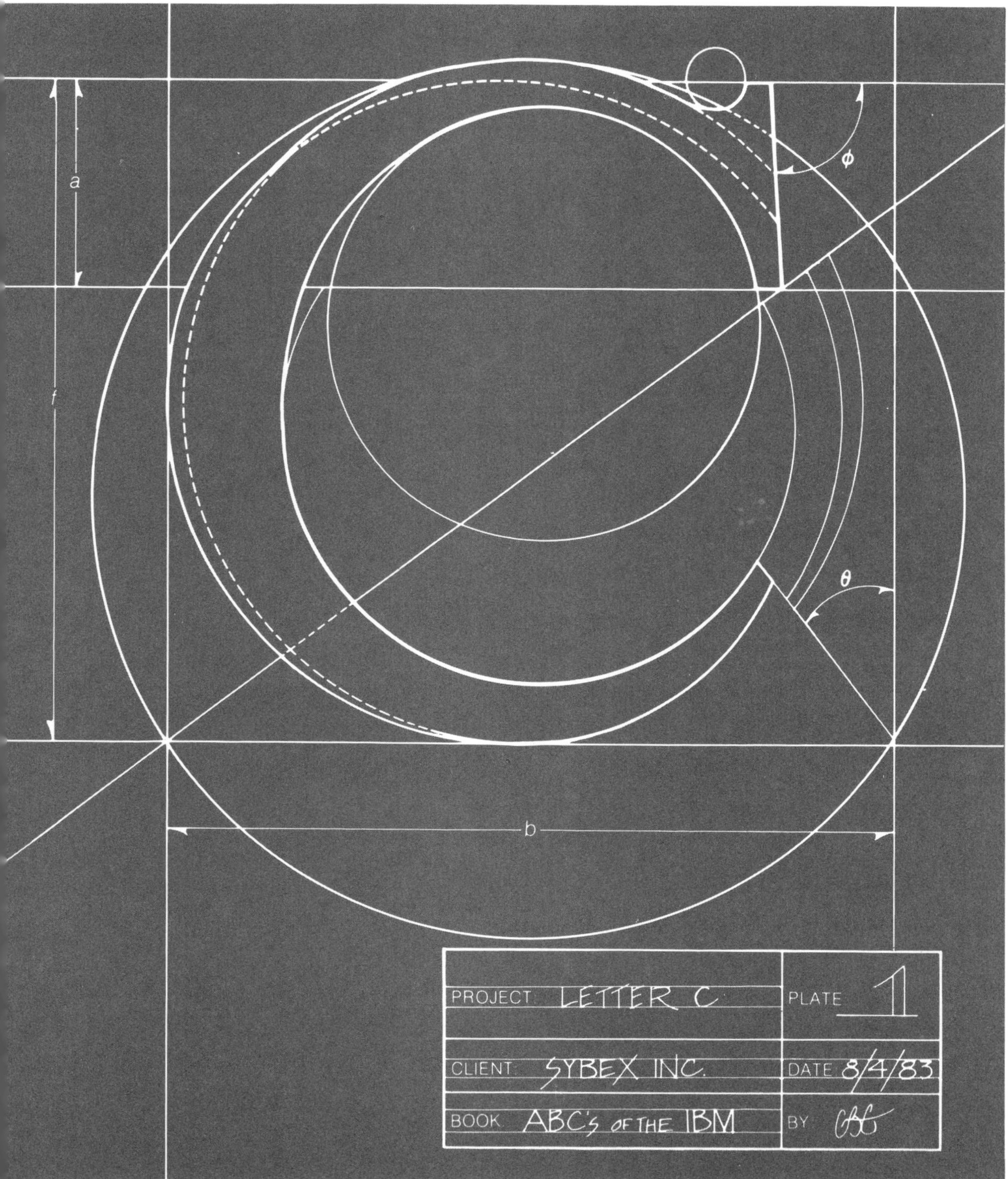
a
f
b
φ
θ
PROJECT LETTER C
PLATE 1
CLIENT SYBEX INC.
DATE 8/4/83
BOOK ABC's OF THE IBM
BY

YOU CHECKLIST

_______ Did you get an error message? Look it up in the back of the appropriate reference manual and follow the recovery steps.

_______ Have you loaded DOS? You cannot do anything until you have.

_______ Did you make a typing mistake? Correct the error and try again.

_______ Are you using the software correctly? Check the appropriate reference manual to be sure there is not some confusion about what you are trying to do.

_______ Are you using the correct file name? Use the DIR command to check the files on the diskette.

_______ Are you using the correct diskette? Again, use the DIR command to list the files.

_______ Does the file name need a drive identifier? If the diskette is not in the current drive, you need to precede the file name with either A: or B:.

_______ Does the file name have an extension? If it does, you have to use it. Use the DIR command to check the complete file name.

_______ Has the diskette been formatted? You cannot store information on a new diskette until you format it using the FORMAT command.

_______ Are you using a defective diskette? Take the diskette out and examine it for chips, bumps, or scratches.

_______ Have you inserted the diskette properly? Make sure it is inside the drive as far as it will go and the drive door is closed.

_______ Did you close the drive door properly? Open and close it just to be sure.

_______ When was the last time you cleaned the diskette drives? Honestly?

_______ Ask someone else to take a look. We're always the last ones to notice when we've made a mistake!

PC CHECKLIST

_______ Turn off the system power and disconnect the power cord from the wall. Always do this before you start investigating cables and connections.

_______ Plug another appliance into the wall outlet to see if the outlet works.

_______ Check that the cable connections for the keyboard and display are securely attached to the system unit. Also check the PC end of the power cord.

_______ Turn the contrast and brightness controls all the way to the right. If they have been turned down accidentally, you may not be able to see anything on the display. You can adjust them again later.

_______ Plug the power cord back into the wall and turn on the system power. The PC will run through its self test, indicated by the following three responses:

- The cursor appears at the top left of the screen.
- You hear a short beep.
- The IBM copyright line is displayed.

_______ If anything other than these three responses occurs, go to the *Guide To Operations* manual. Follow the steps in the section on Problem Determination Procedures (PDPs) to further diagnose the problem.

_______ Ask for help. Two heads are almost always better than one.

SERVICE

If all else fails, you are going to need help from IBM. Find your warranties and check your service contract. The initial warranty covers your PC for 90 days. You can extend the warranty period with a Dealer Service Option for 9 months (nonrenewable) or a full year (renewable annually). If your PC belongs to your company, check to see if they have their own service arrangements.

Make a note of exactly how the problem occurred and any error messages you received. This is important diagnostic information.

For more information, refer to the service information card in the back of the *Guide to Operations* manual.

Appendix A

Putting It All Together

This appendix is for those of you who have just arrived home with your brand new IBM PC. It tells you everything you need to know to put your PC together. We help you choose a good working location and unpack the shipping containers, and then go through the steps for connecting the components.

Before you begin, find a small, flat-blade screwdriver, and notice where there are grounded (3-pin) power outlets to plug your PC into when you are ready to go.

CHOOSING A LOCATION

You need to take some important facts into account when deciding where to set up your PC:

1. Don't pick a place where you will be sitting with your back to a light. The glare of the light on the screen will make it difficult (sometimes impossible) to work.
2. Think about the cables and power cord. Will they be tucked out of the way or will you be inviting someone to trip over them if you put your computer here? Move the PC closer to the wall outlet if necessary.
3. Think about the back of the machine as well as the front. At some point, you will probably need to get at the rear panel—will it be accessible without a major furniture upheaval?
4. Give the PC enough room. The system unit is quite deep and should not be balanced on the edge of a narrow desk. Most people put the keyboard in front of the system unit, so allow space for that too. If you prefer, you can set the keyboard to one side.
5. Give yourself enough room—more than the PC itself occupies. When you start working, you will need space for manuals, papers, diskettes, and perhaps a printer. Choose your working location with this in mind so that things will go smoothly later.

UNPACKING THE SYSTEM UNIT

1. The system unit is in the large, heavy box. Turn the container right side up, cut the binding tape, and open the box.
2. In the cardboard tray on top of the box, you will find the following items:
   - An Inventory Checklist for each item. Since the warranty is printed on the back of the checklists, keep these in a safe place for now and insert them in the *Guide to Operations* manual later.
   - Power cord. Keep this handy—you'll need it in a minute.
   - Two manuals: *Guide to Operations* and *BASIC*. The *Guide to Operations* manual tells you all about operating your PC; the *BASIC* manual tells you how to use the BASIC programming language to program your PC.
   - A plastic bag containing some fact sheets and an IBM customer response card. Put these with the checklists for now and read and complete them later.
3. Having removed these items, take out the cardboard tray.
4. Lift out the system unit. It is tightly packed and quite heavy, so go carefully. Keep all the packing materials in case the system has to be shipped again.
5. Take the system unit out of the plastic bag and place it on a flat surface in your chosen location. You will need access to the rear and enough room to work.
6. Open the diskette drive door(s) and remove the cardboard inserts.
7. Check that the power is off. If you are facing the front of the system unit, the power switch is on the right side of the unit towards the back.

CONNECTING THE KEYBOARD

1. Open the long, flat box that contains the keyboard. Take out the Inventory Checklist/Warranty and keep it in a safe place. Put it in the *Guide to Operations* manual later.

2. Remove the polystyrene packing material, lift out the keyboard, and take it out of its plastic bag. Keep all packing materials.

3. Place the keyboard in front of the system unit. Connect the keyboard cable to the back of the system unit (see Figure A.1). Make sure you push the cable connector on firmly.

CONNECTING THE DISPLAY

1. Turn the display container right side up, cut the binding tape, and open the container.

2. Take out the Inventory Checklist/Warranty and keep it in a safe place. Put it in the *Guide to Operations* manual later.

3. Remove the display. Like the system unit, it is tightly packed, so you will have to struggle a bit. Take off the packing materials and plastic bag and store them with the others.

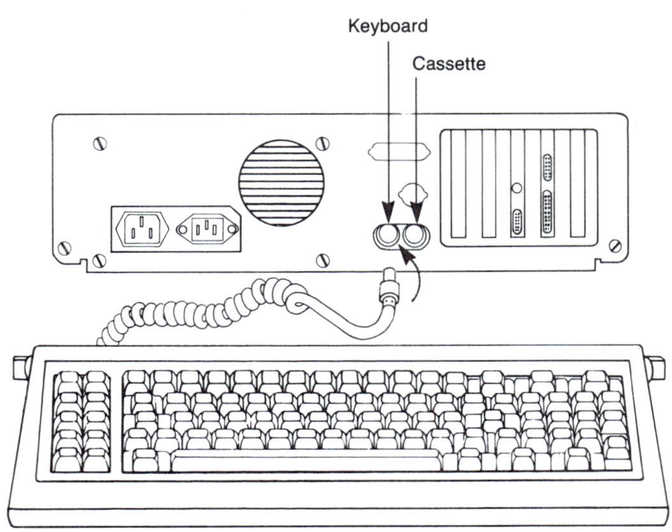

Figure A.1: Connecting the Keyboard

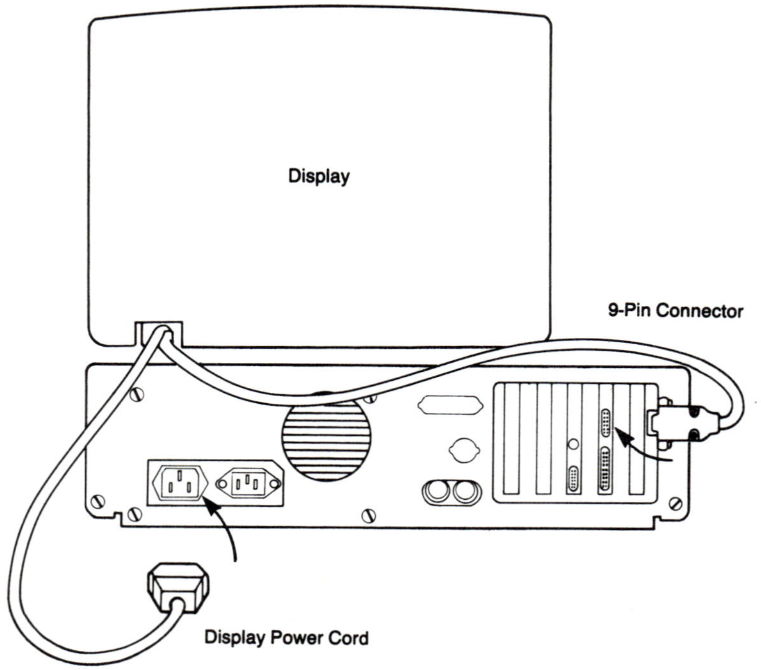

Figure A.2: Connecting the Display

4. Put the display on top of the system unit.
5. Take the plastic bag off the cables on the back of the display.
6. Connect the display cables to the back of the system unit (see Figure A.2). Push both cable connectors on firmly, then tighten the retaining screws on the right-hand connector.

CONNECTING THE POWER CORD

1. Connect one end of the power cord to the back of the system unit (see Figure A.3).
2. Plug the other end of the power cord into a grounded wall outlet.

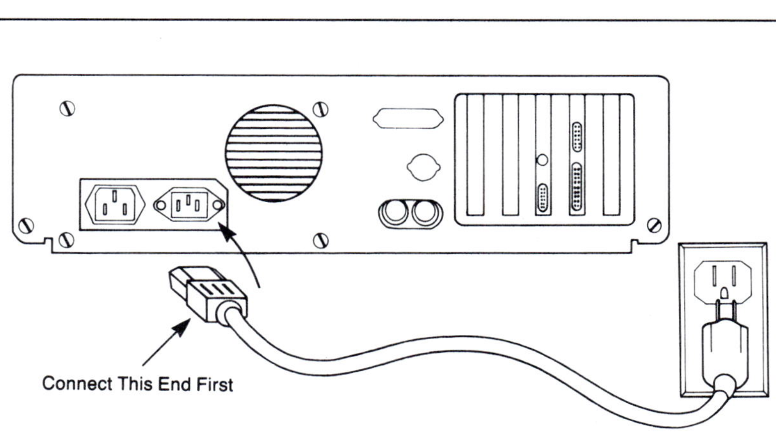

Figure A.3: Connecting the Power Cord

ADJUSTING THE KEYBOARD

The keyboard is designed to be level or to tilt and is adjusted with the knobs on the top corners. Squeeze the knobs in and turn them toward you to tilt the keyboard, away from you to make it level (see Figure A.4). Try it both ways so that you can decide which feels best for you.

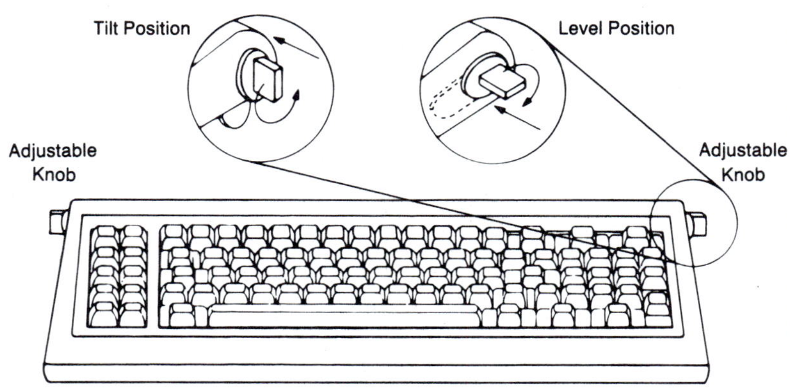

Figure A.4: Adjusting the Keyboard

That's it! Take a minute to make sure your PC is set up in a good location, then go back to *Chapter 1* to find out what all these components do, or to *Chapter 2* where we tell you how to turn on the power and start using your PC.

Appendix B

Using a Single-Drive PC

This appendix gives instructions for using a single-drive PC.

COPYING THE DOS DISKETTE

1. Insert the DOS diskette in the diskette drive and close the drive door.
2. To begin copying the diskette, type:

   A>DISKCOPY

3. Your PC displays the message:

   Insert source diskette in drive A:
   Strike any key when ready

   Since you have already inserted the diskette, press any key to begin the copy operation.
4. The red drive light goes on and you hear a whirring sound. When the information on the diskette has been transferred into memory, you will see:

   Insert target diskette in drive A:
   Strike any key when ready

5. Remove the DOS diskette, return it to its protective sleeve and store it in a safe place.
6. Insert a blank diskette in the drive, close the drive door, and press any key to copy DOS onto this diskette.

Depending on the amount of memory available in your PC, you may have to repeat steps 1 through 6 more than once. If this is the case, DOS will tell you when to change diskettes.

FORMATTING A DISKETTE

1. Load DOS if you haven't already done so.
2. To begin the formatting operation, type:

    A>FORMAT

3. Your PC displays this message:

    Insert new diskette for drive A:
    and press any key when ready

4. Remove the DOS diskette and insert a blank diskette in the drive.
5. Press any key to begin the formatting operation.
6. You will see this message:

    Formatting ...

    followed by:

    Formatting ... format complete
    Format another (Y/N)?

    when the operation is complete.
7. Type *N* since you don't want to format another diskette.
8. Remove the blank, formattted diskette and replace it with the DOS diskette.

MAKING A COPY ON ANOTHER DISKETTE

1. Load DOS if you haven't already done so.
2. To copy the file SPACE.BAS from the DOS diskette in the drive to a file called ASTRO on the diskette you just formatted, type:

    A>COPY SPACE.BAS B:ASTRO

    Remove the DOS diskette, insert the newly formatted diskette, and press ↵.

3. Repeat the procedure to copy all the files from the DOS diskette that begin with E. Remove the diskette you are copying to and insert the DOS diskette. Type:

   ```
   A>COPY E*.*B:
   ```

   Remove DOS and insert the copy diskette. Press ↵.

Appendix C

Glossary: or, A Little Bit of Computerese for the Converted

BACKUP

A backup is a duplicate copy of a file or diskette. When you make such a copy, you are *doing a backup*. Backup a diskette using the DOS DISKCOPY command; backup a file using the DOS COPY command.

BIT

Short for Binary digIT. That tells you a lot, doesn't it! Well, we could go on about binary digits being 0 and 1 and computers operating on ON/OFF signals where ON is 1, and OFF is 0, but, honestly, would you be any the wiser? You might want to remember that there are eight bits in a *byte*, but then again, you might not.

BOOT

When you load the operating system, PC-DOS, you are *booting* your computer. Loading DOS by turning the power on is a *hard boot*; resetting is a *soft boot*.

BUG

Anything that makes the computer or its software stop working as planned. The story goes that an insect trapped inside an early computer caused it to malfunction; little did that insect know it was headed for immortality!

BYTE

The unit of measurement for computer storage and memory. A byte can store about one character of information. Bits and bytes go together; there are eight bits in a byte.

CHIP

Also called a silicon chip. This tiny sliver of silicon, containing incredibly complex circuits, is the heart and soul of your computer and the single technological advance that shrank it to desktop size.

CPU

Short for Central Processing Unit. It is the place in the system unit of your IBM PC where all information is processed. Also known as a microprocessor.

CRASH

A complete malfunction of your computer, much worse than a bug. Originally meant that the read/write head inside the diskette drive had crashed into the diskette, but has now become a generic term for any major breakdown.

CRT

Short for Cathode Ray Tube. The tube itself is a television tube that allows information to be shown on the display screen, but the term is used to refer to computer terminals and displays that use CRTs.

DAISY WHEEL

The kind of print wheel used in many letter-quality printers. It has a central hub and lots of spokes with printable characters on the ends. Looks *something* like a daisy.

DATA

Hardly a computer term any more. Everyone gathers and processes data these days. Really just means information.

DATA BASE

A collection of files that are grouped together because they have something in common. They can be sorted and accessed selectively and thus form valuable sources of information. When you receive junk mail, chances are your name has been pulled out of a large computer data base.

DEBUG

Correcting a hardware or software error—getting the bugs out—is debugging. Sometimes debugging is done by people; sometimes it is done by special software programs.

DEFAULT

Something the computer assumes unless you tell it otherwise. For example, the IBM PC automatically uses the default drive, A:, unless you tell it you want to use drive B:.

DOWNTIME

If your system crashes, it will be out of action, or down, for a while. If the crash occurred at 1:45 pm and the system is not repaired until 4:03 pm the same day, downtime was 2 hours and 18 minutes.

FLOPPY DISK

Another name for a diskette. Sometimes just called a floppy.

FLOWCHART

A sort of road map to a computer program. Programmers design a flowchart to help them write a program. It tells them what should follow what and where to go if a particular event occurs.

HARD COPY

A printed paper copy of anything your computer produces, from a computer program listing to a word-processing document.

HEAD

A small magnetic device inside a diskette drive that reads and writes information on diskettes.

INPUT

Anything you put into your computer—commands, programs, instructions. Your input tells the computer what to do.

INTERACTIVE

When you give your computer an instruction and it responds, you are interacting with each other. Most application programs are interactive.

INTERFACE

A piece of hardware or software that allows communication between your computer and another device. For example, a printer interface lets you transfer information from your PC to a printer.

KILOBYTE

Approximately one thousand bytes (1,024 to be precise), usually abbreviated to Kb or K bytes.

KLUDGE

Everybody has their own definition of this term. For us, it's something that has been put together sloppily in great haste. It's recognizable by wires sticking out and maybe a little smoke. It works, but nobody is sure why. Your IBM PC is *not* a kludge.

LINE FEED

To advance by one line. Most printers have a line feed button that you press to move the paper up by one line.

LINE PRINTER

A high-speed printer capable of printing an entire line at a time. Used with large, shared computers rather than individual personal computers.

LOGGED DRIVE

Another way of saying the current or default diskette drive.

MEGABYTE

A million bytes, usually abbreviated to Mb or M bytes.

MEMORY

The part of the computer that stores programs and information. There are different kinds of memory (see RAM and ROM).

MICROCOMPUTER

A complete, small, computer system, like your IBM PC.

MICROPROCESSOR

See CPU.

NERD

A cross between a human being and a computer. Usually pale and thin with red eyes and a vocabulary consisting only of the terms in this glossary. Also sometimes called a techno-junkie. This is for your edification only—*never* call someone a nerd.

NETWORK

A group of interconnected computers that can communicate and share, send, and receive information among themselves.

OUTPUT

What your computer comes up with after acting on your input. The output may be displayed on the screen, stored on a diskette, or printed, depending on your instructions.

PERIPHERAL

Any additional equipment you attach to your computer. Printers and diskette drives are typical peripherals.

RAM

Random Access Memory—the part of the computer's memory that temporarily holds your program and instructions while you are working with them. When you turn the computer off, RAM loses its memory, and your information along with it, unless you have stored the information on diskette.

READ A DISKETTE

To copy information from a diskette into the computer's memory. You can't use the information stored on a diskette until it has been read into memory.

RESPONSE TIME

The interval between you telling the computer to do something and it acting on your instructions. The shorter the better.

ROM

Read Only Memory—the part of the computer's memory that holds information permanently. With your PC, BASIC is in ROM and is stored there at all times, even if you turn the PC off and go home for the day.

UTILITY

Software used for regularly performed operations. Several steps are combined to carry out a complete operation with only one instruction from you. Makes your life easier, and the computer work for its living.

WRITE TO A DISKETTE

To copy information from the computer's memory onto a diskette. Keeps a permanent copy on diskette for future use—the computer's memory is only temporary.

Appendix D

Resources

IBM MANUALS

BASIC

Provided with your PC. Describes IBM PC BASIC; a reference to all BASIC commands, functions, statements, and variables.

DOS

Provided with the PC-DOS diskette. Introduces you to DOS and how to load it; gives a reference to all the DOS commands with examples of use; explains error messages; provides DOS technical information.

Guide to Operations

Provided with your PC. Describes the components of the PC and how to set them up; introduces you to DOS and BASIC; explains Problem Determination Procedures (PDPs).

Hardware Maintenance and Service

Purchased separately. Includes information on identifying and solving hardware problems, maintenance of your PC, and a parts catalog.

Technical Reference

Purchased separately. Intended for programmers, engineers, or anyone who wants to know how the PC is designed and works; includes technical specifications on all PC hardware.

BOOKS

Practical WordStar Uses, Julie Anne Arca, Sybex, 1983.

An overview of this powerful word processing program, plus boilerplate paragraphs, form letters and documents, two-column and special formats, and other time-saving techniques. Includes WordStar Command Reference Poster.

The VisiCalc Book for the IBM Personal Computer, Donald H. Beil, Reston Publishing Company, Inc., 1983.

For both new and experienced VisiCalc users. Capabilities of VisiCalc; the worksheet; VisiCalc commands; labels, numbers, and formulas; functions; error correction; templates; chapter of practice problems.

Your IBM Personal Computer: Use, Applications and BASIC, David E. Cortesi, CBS College Publishing, 1982.

For the new PC owner. Unpacking and setting up the PC; exercises on using the keyboard, display, printer, and PC-DOS; shopping for programs and supplies; organizing a diskette library; simple programming in BASIC.

VisiCalc for the IBM Personal Computer, Edouard J. Desautels, Wm. C. Brown Company Publishers, 1982.

For those new to computers and VisiCalc. Introduction to the IBM PC; simple VisiCalc problems; functions; complex calculations; file formats; case studies; optional diskette of examples available.

IBM's Personal Computer, Chris DeVoney and Richard Summe, Que Corporation, 1982.

For any potential user of the IBM PC. General interest and technical information; IBM's position in the market; the PC components; additional options; evaluation of available software; service arrangements.

IBM Personal Computer: An Introduction to Programming and Applications, Larry Joel Goldstein and Martin Goldstein, J. Brady Company, 1982.

For the computer novice who wants to program in BASIC. Using BASIC; using data files; computer graphics; word processing; games; programming for scientists; computer simulations; software applications.

Programming the IBM Personal Computer: BASIC, Neill Graham, CBS College Publishing, 1982.

For the new user with no prior programming experience. Explains how to use the features of BASIC to create a program; programming exercises at the end of each chapter; begins with simple programs and builds to more complex examples.

Mastering VisiCalc, Douglas Hergert, Sybex, 1983.

For the beginner. Step-by-step explanations of how to create and use spreadsheets. Many examples, including advanced features.

The IBM PC Guide, James E. Kelley, Jr., Dell/Banbury.

A guide to programming the PC. Includes a diskette of sample BASIC programs and test data files.

IBM PC-DOS HANDBOOK, Richard A. King, Sybex, 1983.

For more experienced users and programmers. Where to find and how to handle the various parts of DOS; how to adapt your PC to meet specific application needs. Appendices include complete memory map; detailed directory and file formats; differences between PC-DOS versions 1.0 and 1.1.

BASIC Exercises for the IBM Personal Computer, J.P. Lamoitier, Sybex, 1982.

For all readers with a minimum technical background. Introduction to BASIC; flowcharts; integers; geometry; data processing; mathematical and financial computations; games; operations research; statistics.

Doing Business with VisiCalc, Stanley R. Trost, Sybex, 1983.

For those with a basic knowledge of VisiCalc who want to know more. More than 40 practical business applications—financial statements, budgets, pricing models, investment strategies.

Using the IBM Personal Computer, T.G. Lewis, Reston Publishing Company, Inc., 1983.

For the new or potential IBM PC owner. Introduction to computers; computer vocabulary; introduction to the IBM PC and PC-DOS; introduction to EasyWriter and word processing; introduction to VisiCalc and spreadsheets; writing your own programs; introduction to data base management; computer technology.

Introduction to WordStar, Arthur Naiman, Sybex, 1982.

For the beginner. Editing; moving and deleting blocks of text; checking copy for accuracy; creating and merging files; on-screen formatting; special print effects. Dictionary of WordStar, SpellStar, and MailMerge commands. Key diagrams.

The Executive's Guide to the IBM Personal Computer: BASIC Programming and VisiCalc, Alan J. Parker, Ph.D., Reston Publishing Company, Inc. 1983.

A written guide and two diskettes of examples, exercises, and problems. Major emphasis on BASIC; less on VisiCalc.

Hands-on BASIC for the IBM Personal Computer, Herbert Peckham, McGraw-Hill, Inc., 1983.

For anyone who wants to learn to program the PC. Introduction to the PC and BASIC; graphics and sound; computer arithmetic and program management; input, output, and simple applications; branching; looping; functions.

The IBM Personal Computer, Robert J. Traister, Tab Books, Inc., 1983.

For the potential IBM PC owner. Development of the IBM PC; information on applications and peripherals; hands-on programming guidance; available software; design characteristics of the PC.

Useful BASIC Programs for the IBM PC, Stanley R. Trost, Sybex, 1983.

A collection of practical programs for calculating home finances, analyzing business and personal investments, investigating real-estate options, and keeping records. No knowledge of BASIC necessary—just enter them into your computer.

DON'T (or How to Care for Your Computer), Rodnay Zaks, Sybex, 1981.

For everyone. Care and maintenance of the computer, diskettes, display, printer, and software. The DOs and DON'Ts of computer use.

Your First Computer, A Guide to Business and Personal Computing, Rodnay Zaks, Sybex, 1983.

For the beginner who wants to know more than just the basics. Understanding, buying, and using small computers for personal and business applications.

User's Handbook to IBM BASIC, Jeffrey R. Weber, Weber Systems, Inc., 1982.

For the new user with no prior programming experience, provides step-by-step instructions in IBM BASIC. For the experienced programmer, provides information on advanced features and a reference guide to all BASIC commands.

MAGAZINES

BYTE, BYTE Publications, Inc.
Monthly; $19/year.
Send subscription inquiries to: BYTE, Subscription Department, P.O. Box 590, Martinsville, NJ 08836.

For the experienced computer user. Articles and information are technical in nature and are intended for the person who wants to know how their computer is put together and what makes it work.

Creative Computing, Ahl Computing, Inc.
Monthly; $24.97/year.
Send subscription inquiries to: Creative Computing, Subscription Department, P.O. Box 789-M, Morristown, NJ 07960. Phone: (800) 631-8112.

For the computer hobbyist. Includes evaluations and profiles, program listings, reviews, and product information.

Dr. Dobb's Journal for Users of Small Computer Systems, People's Computer Company.
Monthly; $25/year.
Send subscription inquiries to: Dr. Dobb's Journal, Subscription Department, P.O. Box E, Menlo Park, CA 94025.

For the computer hobbyist, programmer, or engineer. Includes complete listings of public-domain software, as well as nuts and bolts information on system configuration, compilers, and high-level programming languages.

InfoWorld, Popular Computing, Inc.
Weekly; $25/year.
Send subscription inquiries to: InfoWorld, Subscription Department, P.O. Box 880, Framingham, MA 01701. Phone:(800)343-6474

For all microcomputer users. Software reviews, new product information, book reviews, computer literacy for the novice, industry reports.

Interface Age, Interface Age Magazine, Inc.
Monthly; $21/year.
Send subscription inquiries to: Interface Age, Subscription Department, 16704 Marquardt Avenue, Ceritos, CA 90701.

For the business computer user. Software and hardware reviews, implementation for business use, using application programs, using computers to manage your business.

PC Magazine, Ziff-Davis Publishing.
Monthly; $24.97/year.
Send subscription inquiries to: PC Magazine, Subscription Department, P.O. Box 789-M, Morristown, NJ 07960.

For a general audience. Includes articles on hardware, software, and applications, as well as tutorials for the new user.

PC World, PC World Communications, Inc.
Monthly; $24/year.
Send subscription inquiries to: PC World, Subscription Department, P.O. Box 6700, Bergenfield, NJ 07621.

For a general audience. Includes hardware and software information, software reviews, personality profiles, user-group and bulletin-board updates.

Personal Computer Age, Personal Computer Age Publishing.
Monthly; $24/year.
Send subscription inquiries to: Personal Computer Age, Subscription Department, 10057 Commerce Avenue, Tujunga, CA 91042.

For the sophisticated IBM PC user; content is technical in nature. Regular features include in-depth reviews of software and hardware, a monthly vendor directory, problem reports and solutions, programming techniques, program listings, communications column, new product information.

Personal Computing, Hayden Publishing Company, Inc.
Monthly; $18/year

Send subscription inquiries to: Personal Computing, Subscription Department, 50 Essex Street, Rochelle Park, NJ 07662.

For a general audience. Includes new product information, hardware and software reviews, games, and interviews.

Popular Computing, BYTE Publications, Inc.
Monthly; $15/year.
Send subscription inquiries to: Popular Computing, Subscription Department, P.O. Box 307, Martinsville, NJ 08836.

For the amateur computer hobbyist. Focus is on games and education; also includes new product reviews, editorials, and software bug reports.

Softalk (for the IBM PC), Softalk Publishing, Inc.
Monthly; $24/year; free trial subscription offered to any IBM PC owner (send your serial number).
Send subscription inquiries to: Softalk, Subscription Department, P.O. Box 60, North Hollywood, CA 91603.

For any PC owner; content is a mixture of feature stories, tutorials, and technical information. Regular features include software reviews, new product news, beginners' tutorials, DOS tutorials, question and answer column, software best-seller poll, spreadsheet column, monthly contest.

PUBLIC INFORMATION SERVICES

Public information services offer subscribers the latest news and information from a variety of sources. By adding an asynchronous communications adapter (see *Chapter 8*) and subscribing to the service of your choice, you can turn your PC into an electronic newspaper.

The Dow Jones Reporter

Headlines and news stories from the *Wall Street Journal*, *Barrons*, and the Dow Jones News Service; current market quotes on stocks, bonds, options, and mutual funds. Available from your IBM dealer.

The SOURCE

News from the UPI News Service; stock reports; classified ads; airline schedules; puzzles and games; consumer information. Available from the SOURCE; phone: (703) 734-7500.

USER GROUPS

User groups give you an opportunity to meet and talk with other PC users—ask questions, solve problems, share experiences. Check with your local user group for meeting times and details. The following list, reprinted with permission from *PC World*, Vol. 1, Issue 1, 1983, was current at the time of publication.

Alabama

Birmingham User Group
Chet Ellis
ComputerLand
215 West Valley Avenue
Birmingham, AL 35209
(205)942-8085

Arizona

The Phoenix Personal Computer Club
Fred Lynch
P.O. Box 44218
Phoenix, AZ 95064
(602)266-6634

IBM PC Idea Exchange
Lisa May
United Systems Corporation
1074 E. Sandpiper Drive
Tempe, AZ 85283
(602)831-9363

IBM PC User Group
Theresa Baudier
711 E. River Front Drive
Tucson, AZ 85719
(602)622-4751

California

San Diego Computer Society
John Field
1384 Caliente Loop
Chula Vista, CA 92010
(714)421-9686

IBM Users Group of California
Neil Zachary
P.O. Box 4136
Los Angeles, CA 90028
(213)937-1314

Modesto User Group
Liz Leedom
P.O. Box 1122
Modesto, CA 95353
(209)578-2358

San Francisco IBM PC User Group
Alfred Goodwin
Software Center
4720 Geary Street
San Francisco, CA 94118
(415)751-2231

San Francisco PC Club
Max Brioski
1880 California Street, #12
San Francisco, CA 94109
(415)775-8882

Santa Barbara City College
Computer Science Department
Stu Swartz
721 Cliff Drive
Santa Barbara, CA 93109
(805)966-2919

Silicon Valley Computer Club
Peter Harris
P.O. Box 60506
Sunnyvale, CA 94088
(408)248-9057

Colorado

Denver User Group
Steve Leibson
4040 Greenbriar Boulevard
Boulder, CO 80303
(303)494-4062

Connecticut

The IBM PC User Club of Stamford
Dave Foulger
69 River Street
New Canaan, CT 06840
(203)966-9378

Central Connecticut User Group
Rich Paterson
ComputerLand
131 S. Main Street
West Hartford, CT 06107
(203)561-1446

DC

IBMICRO
Mike Todd
1414-C Wright Circle, Bolling AFB
Washington, DC 20336
(202)433-4380

Washington D.C. User Group
Ted Landberg
13700 Beauwick Court
Silver Springs, MD 20906
(202)275-2102

Florida

Sarasota Chapter of the Autumn Revolution
Saul Lowitt
2131 Brookhaven Drive
Sarasota, FL 33579
(813)921-3230

Idaho

Idaho PC User Group
Bruce Burns
ComputerLand
687 S. Capitol Boulevard
Boise, ID 83702
(208)344-5545

Illinois

Northern Illinois IBM PC Users Group
James L. Szafranski
5195 Castaway Lane
Barrington, IL 60010
(312)934-8133

Indiana

ComputerLand User Group
Susan Shields
ComputerLand
5450 N. Goldwater Road
Fort Wayne, IN 46825
(219)483-8107

Indianapolis IBM User Group
David Reed
6704 Hoover Road
Indianapolis, IN 46260
(317)259-7892

Iowa

Cedar Falls User Group
Lee Ann Moore
Black Hawk Village Shopping Center
Cedar Falls, IA 50613
(319)277-1700

Kansas

Topeka Library User Group
Becky Hinton
Topeka Public Library
1515 W. 10th Street
Topeka, KS 66604
(913)233-2040

Maryland

Lutherville User Group
Bob Roswell
1516 York Road
Lutherville, MD 21903
(301)337-5555

Massachusetts

Miller Microcomputer Services
61 Lakeshore Road
Natick, MA 01760
(617)653-6136

Boston Computer Society/IBM User Group
Michael Rohrbach
P.O. Box 307
Wellesley Hills, MA 02181
(617)235-8830

Minnesota

Minneapolis User Group
Peter LeNeau
100 N. 6th Street, #800A
Minneapolis, MN 55403
(612)239-3233

New Jersey

Personna Computer Association
The International Association for the PC
Paul Cowan
P.O. Box 759
Point Pleasant, NJ 08742
(201)840-0300

New York

The Manhattan IBM Micro Club
Helaine Head
360 Central Park West
New York, NY 10025
(212)222-9027

The New York IBM PC Users Group
Jon Rigo
SYSDOC, Inc.
1385 York Avenue
New York, NY 10021
(212)249-6418

North American Amateur Computer Club
Brian Glasser
P.O. Box 106 Church Street Station
New York, NY 10008
(212)674-1185

North Jersey IBM PC Club
Irving Lang
7 W. 45th Street
New York, NY 10036
(212)581-4667

The Long Island Computer Association
Marvin Freifeld
3 Lindron Avenue
Smithtown, NY 11787
(516)724-0574

Pennsylvania

International Personal Computer Owners
James B. Cookinham
IPCO, Inc.
P.O. Box 10426
Pittsburgh, PA 15234
(412)561-1857

Tennessee

IBM PC User Group
Ross Burrus
Science Applications, Inc.
Plaza Tower #801
Oak Ridge, TN 37830
(615)482-6649

Texas

The IBM Club
David Andrews
3110 Honey Tree Lane
Austin, TX 78746
(512)327-0029

Texas User Group
Rob Taylor
8023 Shady Grove
Houston, TX 77040
(713)937-3592

Dallas Fort Worth User Club
Samuel P. Cook
309 Lincolnshire
Irving, TX 75061
(214)253-6979

Texas User Group
Ken Holcombe
178 Tipperary
San Antonio, TX 78223
(512)333-7163

Canada

Northern Alberta PC User Group
Gerry J. Danen
106 Abbotsfield Road
Edmonton
Alberta T5W 4S9
Canada
(403)474-0732

Index

The SYBEX Library

FOR YOUR IBM PC

THE BEST OF IBM® PC SOFTWARE
by Stanley R. Trost 144 pp., illustr., Ref. 0-104
Separates the wheat from the chaff in the world of IBM PC software. Tells you what to expect from the best available IBM PC programs.

IBM® PC DOS HANDBOOK
by Richard King 144 pp., illustr., Ref. 0-103
Explains the PC disk operating system, giving the user better control over the system. Get the most out of your PC by adapting its capabilities to your specific needs.

BUSINESS GRAPHICS FOR THE IBM® PC
by Nelson Ford 200 pp., illustr., Ref. 0-124
Ready-to-run programs for creating line graphs, complex illustrative multiple bar graphs, picture graphs, and more. An ideal way to use your PC's business capabilities!

THE IBM® PC CONNECTION
by James W. Coffron 200 pp., illustr., Ref. 0-127
Teaches elementary interfacing and BASIC programming of the IBM PC for connection to external devices and household appliances.

BASIC EXERCISES FOR THE IBM® PERSONAL COMPUTER
by J.P. Lamoitier 252 pp., 90 illustr., Ref. 0-088
Teaches IBM BASIC through actual practice, using graduated exercises drawn from everyday applications.

USEFUL BASIC PROGRAMS FOR THE IBM® PC
by Stanley R. Trost 144 pp., Ref. 0-111
This collection of programs takes full advantage of the interactive capabilities of your IBM Personal Computer. Financial calculations, investment analysis, record keeping, and math practice—made easier on your IBM PC.

INTRODUCTION TO COMPUTERS

DON'T (or How to Care for Your Computer)
by Rodnay Zaks 214 pp., 100 illustr., Ref. 0-065
The correct way to handle and care for all elements of a computer system, including what to do when something doesn't work.

YOUR FIRST COMPUTER
by Rodnay Zaks 258 pp., 150 illustr., Ref. 0-045
The most popular introduction to small computers and their peripherals: what they do and how to buy one.

INTERNATIONAL MICROCOMPUTER DICTIONARY
120 pp., Ref. 0-067
All the definitions and acronyms of microcomputer jargon defined in a handy pocket-size edition. Includes translations of the most popular terms into ten languages.

FROM CHIPS TO SYSTEMS: AN INTRODUCTION TO MICROPROCESSORS
by Rodnay Zaks 552 pp., 400 illustr., Ref. 0-063
A simple and comprehensive introduction to microprocessors from both a hardware and software standpoint: what they are, how they operate, how to assemble them into a complete system.

BUSINESS & PROFESSIONAL

COMPUTER POWER FOR YOUR LAW OFFICE
by Daniel Remer 225 pp., Ref. 0-109
How to use computers to reach peak productivity in your law office, simply and inexpensively.

GETTING RESULTS WITH WORD PROCESSING
by Martin Dean & William E. Harding 250 pp., Ref. 0-118
How to get the most out of your SELECT word processing program.

INTRODUCTION TO WORD PROCESSING
by Hal Glatzer 205 pp., 140 illustr., Ref. 0-076
Explains in plain language what a word processor can do, how it improves productivity, how to use a word processor and how to buy one wisely.

INTRODUCTION TO WORDSTAR™
by Arthur Naiman 202 pp., 30 illustr., Ref. 0-077
Makes it easy to learn how to use WordStar, a powerful word processing program for personal computers.

PRACTICAL WORDSTAR™ USES
by Julie Anne Arca 200 pp., illustr., Ref. 0-107
Pick your most time-consuming office tasks and this book will show you how to streamline them with WordStar.